SALT IN THE AIR

The setting is an old Thames barge and the Essex creeks and saltings — haunting, evocative, rich in bird and wildlife. Add in the challenge, adventure and sheer comedy of introducing youngsters to the marvels of sail, life afloat and the great outdoors, the appeal of seeing lives rebuilt with new faith and purpose, and you have a taste of the very special flavour of this book...

The stories themselves are true. Together they record, in part at least, the story of Fellowship Afloat, a very special sailing centre on the Essex coast which offers a new dimension of life to youngsters, especially those from less privileged backgrounds.

Margaret Hillyer, with her husband David, has been closely involved in the work from its early days. For some time she had special responsibility in catering for the groups. More recently she has been involved full-time in the administration. For both Margaret and David — as for many others — Fellowship Afloat has become a way of life.

SALT
IN THE AIR

Stories from a very special sailing centre

Margaret Hillyer
Illustrations by John Kevan

A LION PAPERBACK
Tring · Belleville · Sydney

To David
without whose support
and encouragement
this book would never
have been written;
and to Keith and Gerry
without whom Fellowship Afloat
would not have existed

Copyright © 1985 Margaret Hillyer

Published by
Lion Publishing plc
Icknield Way, Tring, Herts, England
ISBN 0 85648 647 7
Albatross Books Pty Ltd
PO Box 320, Sutherland, NSW 2232, Australia
ISBN 0 87670 657 6

First edition 1985

British Library Cataloguing in Publication Data
Hillyer, Margaret
    Salt in the air.
    1. Fellowship afloat
    2. Title
    796'.0941   GV191.48.G7
ISBN 0 85648 647 7

Printed and bound in Great Britain
by Cox & Wyman

Contents

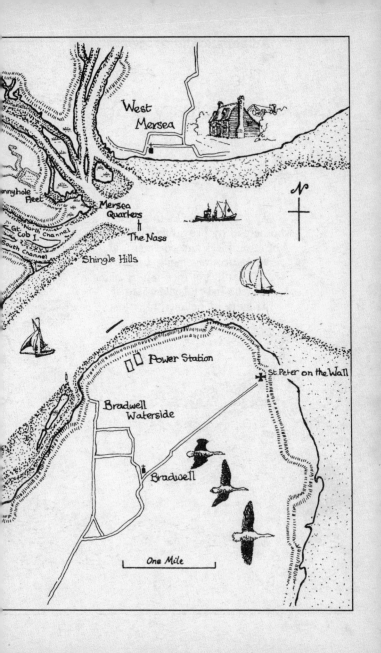

Author's acknowledgement

My grateful thanks to all those
who helped by providing information,
offering ideas and comment, and
giving encouragement. I am only
sorry I could not mention by name
all who have played a part in
the story of Fellowship Afloat.

In at the Deep End

Whatever was I doing, soaking wet and freezing cold, scared stiff and about to heave up over the side of my bunk?

I was dimly aware of the creaking and groaning of this old boat, affectionately called *Odd Times*, as she was tossed about on gigantic waves, while I struggled to convince my stomach that we were floating gently up the familiar Essex creek to Tollesbury.

All around me was chaos and noise. Everything movable down below had already crashed to the lowest level, or so I thought until the next bang came, louder than any previous one.

I did not really care what was happening on deck. I'd given up trying to guess the reason for each sound long ago. I concentrated on lying still, with the occasional apprehensive look through the open hatch, and hoped the boat would not change tack, because if that happened the water would pour down the sail straight onto my bunk — and I would have to struggle to the bunk on the other side, clear the water from it and lie down again.

I should have realized what we were in for when we set out from Westcliff that morning. We had spent the most dreadful night, anchored in a very exposed position, with a south-westerly wildly tossing the boat around. Why we had bothered to tidy up the mound of pots and pans, the teapot and the heap of belongings that had found their way to the cabin floor, I do not know. It was all back there now, with more besides.

No one had wanted to get up and face the horrible mess. The skipper was the only one who surfaced, to tune in to the shipping forecast — remembering too late that it was an hour earlier on Sundays. There was grim determination on everyone's face as the decision was made to sail anyway. Anything would be better than waiting for the next tide on what felt like the back of a bucking bronco.

How I wished I could get off the boat!

'Get yourself togged up and come on deck,' the others said encouragingly. 'You'll feel much better if you are busy.'

It sounded convincing, but I could not stay upright long enough to get into my waterproofs, harness and life-jacket. I managed to prop myself up in the hatch, to see what was going on. But it was obvious that without a harness to clip myself onto the boat a novice like me could quite easily slip overboard.

The conversation on deck did not fill me with confidence.

'South storm cone on the pier,' remarked John, the skipper, as he waved to the coastguards on duty.

'What do you think? Shall we keep going?' asked Rob, our navigator.

'Anything's better than staying here, I reckon.'

I gathered that our journey home would take us through the maze of channels, spitways and sandbanks of the Thames Estuary. Because of our deep draught, we would have to be through the Swin Spitway by 5 p.m. at the latest — after that there would not be enough water.

John and Rob had calculated that we had to make nine knots. With a wind force 7-8, the engine flat out and a spring tide ebbing under us, we should just make it.

I glanced around the deck. It was littered with tyre fenders, warps and heaving-lines — plus a ladder! Even I recognized that this was most unseamanlike. It was also most unlike our skipper, who was very fastidious as a rule. But there was no time to tidy up if we were to make the Swin.

I gave up the struggle and retired to my bunk, convinced that, even if we reached the Swin intact, we would most likely smash to pieces trying to get through.

In the moments when I was not fully preoccupied with

William Emily

exerting my will over the feeling in my stomach, I thought about my crewmates. They so obviously loved *Odd Times* and had great faith in her ability to survive anything. They seemed to enjoy everything to do with boats, especially the old-style, traditional ones. And they were passionately involved in a sailing centre run by a group called 'Fellowship Afloat'. That had had a lot to do with how I came to be on board...

Odd Times, more properly called *William Emily*, was a twenty-ton oyster fishing-smack, rebuilt in the yard at Tollesbury about a hundred years ago. Local story had it that they used spare wood left over from other jobs and the work was carried out at odd times — hence her nickname. She was

11

'traditional' in every sense of the word; and that meant a lot of hard work and constant maintenance.

The decks leaked. Food dropped would disappear without trace into the bilges. And life on board was conducted amongst a welter of gear — everything from paint pots and canvas, to wire, shackles and bottles of linseed oil. There were always ropes needing to be spliced. And there were the permanent hazards of tar on the decks, diesel oil from the engine and the traditional dressing of red ochre and fish oil used on the flax sails.

The sails themselves were very heavy. As well as the weight of the mainsail, there was also the weight of the gaff (the wooden 'boom' attached to the top of the sail) to pull up the mast.

White flannels and spotless deck-shoes were certainly out of place on this boat. Within minutes of stepping on board each of us looked and smelled like an old gaffer, the affectionate nickname given to the original owners of these individual boats.

It was not the lure of the sea, or the promised excitement of a race up the Thames competing with other old smacks like the *William Emily*, which had persuaded me to spend a week on board. The invitation had come from David, the Warden of Fellowship Afloat. He had already introduced me to the Essex mud and the joy of boats at Tollesbury: in particular to an ex-Thames sailing barge called *Memory*.

To tell the truth, I did not need much persuasion to spend time with David. But I was very apprehensive about sailing on *William Emily*. I knew so little about boats and felt so useless, especially since the rest of the crew were keen sailors and always seemed to know what to do.

I had met John, the skipper, before. He was a quietly-spoken, thoughtful guy, who seemed to know what he was about, but had a nice way of sharing with us all, so that even I felt involved with what was happening. Tim I knew to be an experienced racing-dinghy sailor. He was very at home on the smack and had lots of ideas about tuning the rigging and sail technology. David was the ship's carpenter and cook. Sally seemed to know all about sailing. So too did Marion, a medical student who was sailing with us as far as Westcliff, where we would be taking Rob, another experienced sailor, on board. I seemed to be just 'David's friend'.

That first evening I entered into a whole new world. First we took all our gear and provisions out to the smack. Then, after we had stowed everything away, we motored up into the marina to fill up with fuel and water, before dropping back to our mooring to prepare our evening meal. Even I could help with the cooking and washing-up, and there was a lovely feeling of camaraderie as we were all busy about various tasks — from a spot of last-minute eye-splicing, to juggling pots and pans on two burners and a grill. Cooking and menu planning on board was certainly an art.

After an ample repast, we sat about on deck, contented and at peace, gently moving on the water and watching the sun go down. Below, in the saloon, with the Tilly lamp hissing, I could understand why everyone loved *William Emily* and why she was so important to Fellowship Afloat. There's something really cosy and intimate about being huddled together on board, drinking hot chocolate, munching toast and chatting about all kinds of things. The feeling of togetherness made it easy for us to share with one another our faith in the God who had made all this. As we reluctantly went to bed, I was very glad to be part of things.

It was not easy to sleep. There seemed to be so many strange noises, and the gentle, rocking motion of the boat I found disturbing once I was in bed. All too soon there was the sound of the kettle going on for morning tea, and I was surprised to find that it was in fact quite late.

About mid-day we left our mooring, to take the flood tide down to the Thames. As we chugged down past Cob Island, we began to get the sails up. A lot of sheer muscle power was needed, so I was able to feel useful. The vibration of the engine did not help the way my tummy felt and I was glad when John said we could do without it. It was a strange, unaccustomed feeling to be moving over the waves in this old wooden boat, listening to the water against the hull and getting acclimatized to the rolling motion. The whole boat seemed to be complaining as it creaked and groaned.

Before long we were losing sight of land and it was necessary to plot our course carefully. It was exciting to steer a course by the deck compass but hard work to hold the tiller, and I soon grew tired when it was my turn.

Gradually the storm-clouds gathered. We all put on harnesses and life-jackets as our quiet sail became noisier by the minute, with the deck slanting at a peculiar angle. The rain beat in our faces and the wind buffeted us, but I was amazed to see that everyone was actually enjoying it.

I concentrated on not feeling ill, tried to show an interest in the Montgomery wreck and the colour of the buoys that marked her whereabouts, and kept one eye on the changing colour of the sky. Every so often, as the bows crashed down into a trough, there was a loud smack and spray flew all over the deck.

Suddenly we were in the middle of a squall — and there was panic as the mainsheet block parted from the stern sheet bench. Everyone sprang into action except me — I felt it best to keep well out of the way — and soon a makeshift repair was lashed up. Was this the 'joy' of sailing — being wet and cold, feeling sick and wishing that safe, dry land was not so far away?

At Westcliff Rob joined the crew.

'I just managed to persuade my doctor that I could come,' he said. 'I've had glandular fever, but he says he thinks I'll be all right if I take things easy.'

'Not much chance of that around here,' said John.

With our crew complete and the tide with us once more, we set sail for Gravesend and the start of the race. We dropped anchor for the night, relieved to see one or two smacks around the steam-tug *Brent* which would accompany the race.

Next morning, when we went on deck, the fog was so thick we could not see anything. The forecast said it would lift, but it showed no signs of doing so. The race had been due to start at half past seven, but there was no point in moving until we could see where we were going, and we rightly concluded that the start would be delayed.

At last the fog lifted enough for us to see the Committee

Boat chugging in and out of sight, issuing instructions. It seemed obvious that nothing was going to happen for a while. So we settled down to have our breakfast. Then a voice hailed us and announced we were starting at 9.30 a.m. That gave us only fifteen minutes to get ready. By the time we had got ourselves sorted, motored back past the starting-line, organized our sails and come up to the line, it was 9.45 a.m. We must have been the last boat to start.

In the silence of the misty river we could hear sounds which could have been the gear on other boats. But with only forty yards' visibility, we were a bit apprehensive.

However, as we sailed up Fiddler's Reach to Greenhithe, the fog lifted and we could make out the sails of the smacks in front of us. Tim decided that we needed a water sail to make us go faster, so he dug out an old foresail and managed to rig it with help from Rob and David. But nothing we could do made any real difference. Our heavy flax sails and a dirty bottom were rather a handicap, and certainly no match for the terylene ghosters and topsails in front of us.

I found it fascinating to observe London from the river. First the flat, eerie marshland on either side of the river — the Erith marshes whose very name conjured up mystery and bleakness — then past Woolwich into dockland, with miles of dead wharves and warehouses, and silent cranes keeping watch over the passing river traffic.

It was fascinating, too, to keep an eye on the chart and read off all the 'reaches' as we sailed up them: Long Reach, Erith Rands, Erith Reach, Halfway Reach, Barking, Gallion's, Woolwich, Bugsby's, Blackwall, Greenwich, and then into Limehouse Reach, where a most exotic smell of spices wafted across, transporting our senses to some Far Eastern river.

We were almost certainly last at the finish at Cherry Garden Pier, off Deptford, but there was so much activity we did not have time to mind. Now we could actually see the dozen or so smacks that had taken part in the race, as we all mustered in the Pool of London, just below Tower Bridge. We waited impatiently for the bridge to go up and let us all through to moor outside Billingsgate fish market. Eventually the traffic on the bridge stopped and the two sides parted and slowly rose, as if by magic. As we saw the tide rushing through, John began to panic as he considered our approach.

But this was soon forgotten as we watched with horror the manoeuvres of our Royal Naval minesweeper escort, which had gone first through the bridge. As she nosed into HMS *Belfast* to get a line aboard and swing the stern round, it was obvious that there was going to be an almighty bang. A small figure was seen to dash forward at the bows with an enormous fender but it was too late, and several figures pitched forward as the large vessel was brought to a rather abrupt halt. The 'smackies', not too impressed with HM Navy, proceeded to negotiate the bridge and tie up without error. We prayed that we would do likewise.

It was our day for being last! When we had finally satisfied John that all was safe with *William Emily*, we went ashore for our feast of Guinness and oysters in Billingsgate. We were so far behind everyone else that a policeman demanded to know where we were going. Why he could not guess, I do not know, for we were covered in red ochre and could only have come from an old fishing-smack. There were still plenty of oysters left, but after chewing one and swallowing another, I decided that they were not for me. David, who adores shellfish of any kind, had a veritable feast.

Soon we were back on board, getting ready to go under Tower Bridge again, and pass through the lock into St Katharine's Yacht Haven, where we had booked a berth for the night. It was quite an exciting entry because of the strong tide. And we were squashed into the lock with several other boats and hardly room to move. David, eager to take a line ashore, jumped a little too soon, missed the pontoon and was suddenly up to his neck in inky black water.

After that, showers seemed a good idea to everyone, and soon we were all getting rid of the familiar red ochre. It poured from my head like blood. Restored to normality, we headed for the West End to have a meal in style — quite a contrast to the past few days.

A good night's sleep, with only the sounds of lapping water, and no movement, made us glad that we had opted for the extra expense of a sheltered berth, and not tied up alongside a buoy in the river, as some of the smacks had done.

Saturday morning dawned with bright sunshine, and for the first time it was really hot. John, David and I tramped off to see if we could find somewhere to buy food. Eventually we found an East End market, which had all we needed. We hurried back, to be ready to lock out on top of the morning tide and sail back down the Thames.

It was quite a long haul round to Westcliff where we arrived by early evening. Wearily we took to our bunks, dreaming of romantic trips up the Thames and wishing that we did not have to sail back to Tollesbury next day...

A crack so loud I thought that the mast had broken brought me back to the present. What happened, I wondered, if the boat sank? I knew we had a life-raft, but I did not fancy being in it. Surely, I thought, God would not allow anything to happen to this old boat, or to us on board? She played such an important part in Fellowship Afloat, and I had savoured first-hand the joy of being on board and sharing with other people.

I could hear a sail thrashing madly up above, louder than the rain and the wind together, but we were obviously still sailing. After what seemed an eternity, things became calmer and I ventured to poke my head through the hatch to see what had been going on.

If there had been chaos on deck before, the scene now was one of devastation. The loud crack I had heard was the jib ripping in two. The mainsail had also started to tear under the strain.

'Where are we?' I asked. 'Are we through the Spitway?'

'Yes, ages ago,' replied David. 'We're safe now. It won't be long before we are home. We've just seen the inshore lifeboat going out; the crew waved. We're a long way out from the Blackwater, so I don't know where they are heading.'

'Does that mean someone's in trouble?' I asked.

'I should imagine so,' answered David. 'We're lucky it's not us. You missed a great sail, though.'

He told me we had come through the Swin Spitway with minutes to spare, and thick squalls of rain obscuring the buoys which pointed the way through the barely-submerged sandbanks. Our trust in Rob's navigation was well placed.

I went back to my bunk and slept for the last part of our passage. When I awoke, we had dropped our anchor. I had survived my first real voyage. I had come to know, and to respect, *William Emily*'s crew. I wanted to know more, not just about sailing, but about the Fellowship Afloat adventure which had brought them all together and filled them with such obvious enthusiasm.

2

Early Days

'Come on, Gerry, we're going to Tollesbury,' Keith said excitedly to his wife, as he put the phone down. 'Mickey's found us a boat!'

'What sort of a boat?' asked Gerry.

'We'll see when we get there. Come on! He said he'd meet us at half past.'

Although Keith and Gerry did not realize it at the time, this one little phone call was really the beginning of Fellowship Afloat. As they drove to Tollesbury, they reflected upon how this thriving Essex village and its waterside had increasingly attracted them.

The east coast was very different from the Devon coast, where Keith had done most of his sailing. Instead of cliffs and clear water, it was mostly mudbanks and murky water, which never seemed to be there because the tide was always out. But the salt-marshes, covered when the tide was up, exposed as it ebbed, had their own unique character, which was always fascinating.

Keith would have been interested in any place where there were boats and, as he and Gerry visited Tollesbury regularly in the first months of their marriage, they found themselves irresistibly drawn to every new facet that the area revealed to them. Each visit strengthened their dream of buying an old boat, doing it up and sharing it with the group of young people back home with whom they were involved.

On the phone, Mickey had sounded very sure that he had found just the boat they were looking for and, as they drove into Tollesbury, Keith and Gerry were bubbling with expectancy. Soon they were trudging around the sea-wall with Mickey and down onto the saltings, until at last he stopped next to a derelict old fishing-smack, so run-down she was barely recognizable as such. Her name was *William Emily* and Mickey was sure that they could buy her.

She looked very sad, sitting in her mud-berth. Any boat sitting in a mud-berth can look sad, especially when the tide is out and the boat is right down on the mud, hidden below the top of the saltings, patiently waiting for the tide to return and float her. It is amazing how different boats look when the tide comes up, and they sit proudly on the water. However, it would take more than a high tide to make *William Emily* look anything but forgotten and dejected.

In fact it was to take a lot longer than Keith and Gerry ever imagined before she proudly sailed up the creek. But as they looked at her now they were full of plans for restoring her. It was just the sort of thing youngsters would enjoy working at, and one day there would be the reward of taking her to sea.

So they set about persuading the owner to sell, and a friend of theirs to put up the money. Such was their enthusiasm that soon the boat was purchased and boys from the church youth group at Harlow were coming down regularly to slave away at the unenviable task of clearing out all the rubbish and gear that had been dumped inside, and removing the 'ballast', in order to get at the bilge to clean and repair it.

The 'ballast' consisted of pig iron set into concrete, and it all had to be picked out. It was laborious, heavy, dirty work and seemed to go on for ever. Once out on deck, it all had to be got ashore.

It could be carried across wobbly planks from ship to shore. A more sophisticated method was to use the derrick to swing it ashore bit by bit. This was fine until someone got their knot-work wrong and then, of course, the load fell into the mud.

By this time Gerry herself was carrying a fair amount of 'ballast', as she was expecting her first baby. But this did not stop her working as hard as the rest.

Apart from cleaning the boat and fitting-out down below, there was the daunting task of re-rigging. Some of the

William Emily's gear was on board, but most of it seemed to be missing, including her bowsprit. Then one day a conversation with her previous owner revealed that a lot of items must be lying forgotten in one of the boatyards. An eager exploration soon revealed all kinds of treasures and, most exciting, the missing bowsprit.

With renewed determination the work carried on, and an increasing number of people became interested. Other groups of young people, from Chelmsford and Southend, became involved and the vision began to grow. The old fishing-smack was rather small for the average-sized youth group, but there was also canoeing and dinghy sailing, interests which Keith and Gerry firmly believed could be used to help present and challenge young people with some of the deeper issues of life.

One day, after their daughter Anna was born, Keith and Gerry were taking a break from work and calming a fractious baby with a soothing pram-ride across the marshes, when they came across a 140-foot schooner which had been converted into a house-boat. It was up for sale.

'Hey, that's just what we need!' said Keith. 'It's got character, accommodation — it's even got electricity. Much better than a land base.'

'But it would cost thousands, surely?' said Gerry.

'So would a land base. No, this is just what we want — it's ideal. We must find out who owns it and tell everyone about it.'

When they got home Gerry sent out a letter under the heading 'Fellowship Afloat', to as many people as they thought would be interested, asking for support.

Their hopes were quickly dashed when the schooner was sold to someone else. It was hard to understand, as those who were closely involved had become so out of Christian commitment, and they had felt so sure that this idea was one God wanted them to act on. Their own interest in boats, the idea of using a boat for accommodation and dinghies for sailing, the interest and support from friends, all seemed so right. Yet now the boat that had seemed ideal had disappeared under their noses.

About this time application was made for the organization to become a Charitable Trust. Meanwhile work continued on the smack, often in the cold and wet, and although it was reasonably cosy, huddled together down below round the fire, it was hard not to be despondent. It was only their trust in God which kept them going.

Then in the early spring, when Anna was just over a year old, someone spotted a 'For Sale' notice on an old Thames sailing barge lying up the river at Millbeach. All her rigging and gear had been removed and she looked at first sight little more than a rotting hulk.

Despite this, a very excited group of people went out to view her. She was fitted out down below with accommodation for twenty-two, and had been used by the East Coast Sail Trust to take people sailing up and down the east coast until about two years before. She looked a bit neglected and obviously needed a fair bit of work to make her habitable once more. Her price was £850. Her name was *Memory*.

They knew she was the boat they had been looking for. Everything about her appealed. She was old. She had a long history of cargo-carrying and of winning barge matches. She had both atmosphere and character. Thames sailing barges were such a familiar part of the east coast scene. In their heyday they had sailed right up to Tollesbury. *Memory* was much, much better than the schooner. Already they could see her moored in the creek.

But where could they find that amount of money? It seemed impossible. But they were so sure that this was the right boat for the work they believed God was leading them to begin, that they scraped together the £50 needed for a deposit there and then.

'We must write and tell everyone,' said Keith. He was already getting carried away, replanning some of the accommodation and working out how *Memory* could be brought round to Tollesbury.

So the second letter headed 'Fellowship Afloat' went out the very next day.

Next morning, when Keith went downstairs, there was a letter on the doormat with an unfamiliar postmark. Opening it, he found a cheque inside from someone who knew nothing about *Memory*.

'Look, we've got our first gift towards *Memory* — £80,' he called to Gerry upstairs.

'But no one can have received the letter yet!' Gerry said excitedly. 'Let me see.'

Next minute Keith nearly jumped out of his skin as Gerry shrieked, 'Keith, it's not for £80; it's for £800. It's every bit we need!'

'It can't be! Let me look.'

'It is! It's the whole amount,' insisted Gerry.

'I don't believe it! I can't believe it!' Keith stared at the cheque in amazement. How could they doubt, now, that God was really in this work, that he wanted Fellowship Afloat to become a reality, and that *Memory* was part of his plan? As Keith phoned round to share the news, confidence grew.

It was not long before a mooring had been secured for *Memory* and plans were made for towing her round to Tollesbury.

By now the *William Emily* was fairly seaworthy and her engine was in good working order. A lot of work still remained to be done, especially on the rigging, but she would be ideal to provide the tow. Tide-tables were read, the day for moving was decided, and all the preparations were made. It would take two tides to complete the move, so everyone would have to stay on board for one night.

In the event, the last mooring on the barge just would not budge and the smack, which drew a lot more water than *Memory*, had to leave the creek and wait in the deeper water.

At last *Memory* was pulled and poled out of the creek to join *William Emily*. The tide was disappearing fast by this time and after much quanting with the old barge sweeps (rather like long oars) it was decided to anchor off Northey Island and spend the night there.

As the tide went out, the mudbanks began to dry, giving a whole new atmosphere to the area. Then, to everyone's horror, the smack, aground on one of these mudbanks, began to tip over. No one had known there were all these huge hummocks of mud at low water, and it was a great relief when *Memory* stayed afloat and *William Emily* appeared to be surviving.

It was a bit primitive on board, but Keith and Gerry and some of the rest of the 'crew' were seasoned campers.

Everyone was up bright and early the next morning, waiting for enough of a tide to float the smack. Eventually the two boats were lashed together and the strange journey up-river began.

On approaching the creek leading to *Memory*'s new home the barge was cast adrift by the smack, with a 'You can make it on your own now.'

Keith's brother, Stuart, leapt ashore pretty smartly with a rope, and the others grabbed the sweeps, pushing against the sides of the creek to manoeuvre the barge further in.

The creek opened out into a lagoon of water (or mud) in the saltings. This was where *Memory* was to stay. It was a great relief to get her temporarily moored in this lovely quiet spot.

There were many times during the next twelve months when everyone wished it were not quite such an isolated position, so far from the road and the village. It was a good walk around the sea-wall to reach *Memory*, and everything had to be carried: food, water, paraffin for lights, Elsan fluid for the toilet, any wood, materials or tools needed for repair work. And when Keith and Gerry came there was also the pram, with Anna in it.

Even though it was still fairly primitive down below, groups of youngsters came down and stayed on board from the start, happy to do some of the most horrible jobs, for the privilege of being together and sharing everything. Even then, *Memory* had a unique atmosphere, providing a community feeling which broke down barriers, and made us all thankful to God for his provision and love.

The first summer was unforgettable! There was an enormous amount of work that needed doing, the ever-present problem of the barge sinking and always needing to be pumped out (using the old clapper pumps), the excitement of acquiring a couple of dinghies and actually being able to go for a sail as a relief from work, the constant struggle to victual the barge. Everyone's arms grew in length and muscle. Enthusiastic visitors, young and old, large and small, pregnant and otherwise, tottered across the gang-plank in a never-ending stream. And there was constant encouragement, as so many people cheerfully gave their time and energy to the project.

In contrast to all the activity was the peace and tranquillity, the ever-changing scene of the marshes at different stages of tide and in different seasons. It was a good feeling to sit on deck with the sun shining, the smell filling one's nostrils, and the mud popping like fizzy lemonade, silent only when the tide covered it once more.

All too soon winter closed in and *Memory* saw fewer visitors. The workers concentrated on the smack's dinghy, with someone trying to visit *Memory* every week to check that she was all right and to pump out the bilges. One day in late winter, Keith realized that no one had been near *Memory* for a fortnight. So, despite the wind and the cold and the rain, he tugged on his foul-weather gear and set off for Tollesbury. A brisk, bracing walk around the sea-wall made him forget the inclement weather as he dreamed of warmer days and made plans for *Memory*.

As he crossed the gang-plank he was relieved to see that she seemed to be all right. He lifted the hatch — and looked down upon a shiny blackness. To his horror he realized the water was right over the kelson: *Memory* had taken in a good three feet and the bottom bunks would be under water, not to mention the toilet. What a mess!

After two hours' hard work on the clapper pumps Keith no longer felt the cold. He was absolutely exhausted, and he had made no visible impression on the water level.

As he returned around the sea-wall to muster help, he determined that somehow the Fellowship must find enough money to buy a pump and batteries. On arriving home he phoned the other trustees who gave the go-ahead to spend the last of the funds on a small submersible pump and two batteries. Within a couple of hours of being rigged up, it had pumped the barge dry.

This incident led to renewed efforts to find a more convenient mooring and just at this time a lovely big, comfortable berth became available alongside the Gridiron

Pier. In the good old days when the Thames barges visited Tollesbury, they would either go right up the creek to the granary, or they came alongside this pier, which used to be a lot higher than it is now, to unload their cargoes. In those days there was a path which stood up above the high tide, for taking the goods to the road, but it had long since fallen into disrepair.

On the inside of the pier were scrubbing-blocks. Barges could come up on the tide, stop here, and then their skippers could get at the bottom for repairs and cleaning when the tide was out. These scrubbing-blocks were now very silted up, but would provide a very comfortable berth for *Memory*, tucked behind what was left of the pier. She was right on the edge of the saltings with excellent access to the water, so there would be nearly three hours either side of the high tide to sail in the dinghies. It seemed that once more God had made the perfect provision.

3

New Life in Old Timbers

Every weekend saw a group of people eagerly making their way down the path, ankle-deep in mud, carrying an assortment of things — from containers full of water and mounds of tinned food to crow-bars, shovels, paint-pots and saws.

The excitement of getting the barge 'shipshape' and ready to receive 'real' groups spurred people on to work together at painting the cabins, refitting the galley, securing the gang-plank, gathering an assortment of dinghies together and telling others what it was all about.

This was perhaps the most difficult. When someone asks, 'What is Fellowship Afloat?', a thousand-and-one answers spring to mind. It is an old Thames sailing barge called *Memory* out in the middle of an Essex salt-marsh; it is living and working together — peeling the spuds; it is learning to sail and enjoying each other's company; it is the hiss of Tilly lamps and voices singing to a guitar; it is time to sit and stare at salt-marsh, sea and boats — and time to listen; it is an opportunity to realize that God is interested in each person and what he or she is doing; it is learning that God is real and he is *there* — not just in church, but out on the water, in the boat. He is where we are.

Keith and Gerry had real vision in those early days. The

opportunity to sail was not open to everyone, and Keith had so valued his early adventures on boats down in Devon and had thrilled to the excitement it provided. Fellowship Afloat would be somewhere for youngsters to come and learn to sail, to meet the challenge of wind and waves, and something more. Just as the crew learn to trust the skipper and to obey certain rules for everyone to be safe in the boat, so there is a God who will lead us and who has laid down basic guidelines, for our good.

Memory's old timbers were certainly seeing new life. When she was built, a master and a mate would have been the only crew on board, and her sides must have nearly burst with the huge cargoes of coal, fertilizer, manure or grain which filled the great hold. She would have exchanged a load of grain in London for a load of manure to take back to Ipswich, and the master and his boy would have handled the huge sails and lee-boards using winches, strength and skill. They had to hope that the wind would be favourable, for there was no engine to help them out of a tight spot. Their home was the master's cabin, where everything had its place in cupboard or drawer, and getting into bed was like crawling into a cupboard in the wall.

The master's cabin is still there, a living museum-piece a little apart from the rest of the boat. In the years since *Memory* was bought the hold space has been turned into cabins, a saloon and galley, and there is ample accommodation for twenty-two. What fresh secrets *Memory* could now tell, as youngsters lie in their bunks and talk, or sit up late in the saloon over toast and hot chocolate, someone strumming a guitar in the background, or enjoy a chat on deck in the moonlight, watching the marshes by night, looking up at the big sky full of stars and listening to the call of the redshank...

The early work parties soon became real groups as word spread, and people came from different churches and schools to enjoy sailing in the dinghies and doing their bit towards making *Memory* habitable.

Living on board a creaky old boat was fun, even if it did leak and smell musty. And the atmosphere created by the hiss of Tilly lamps in the saloon of a boat steeped in history,

was quite special and had a profound effect on visitors. So too did the fact that the group who ran the place were Christians who believed that God had given them the boat to use for his work.

It was exciting when the first groups booked in to use the barge for a sailing holiday, instead of it being just friends coming down to do some work. Everyone made a special effort to have things ready and, as the word spread, more and more groups wanted to come.

Each Friday evening a small group of people would open up the barge and try to get it habitable: letting out musty smells, filling water-tanks, pumping out. There would be food to collect, and toilets to organize, as well as lighting a fire to get rid of the lingering dampness. If some groups could have seen the situation two hours before they arrived to a nice fire, glowing Tilly lamps, and a mug of hot chocolate, they would never have come.

During the introductory talk there would be much activity up in the fo'c'sle or out on the pontoons, as gear for the boats was sorted over and any damage repaired. All this became a way of life for Keith, Gerry and the others who shared their vision.

Cooking for from fifteen to twenty people on a little domestic gas cooker was an art. For some reason toad-in-the-hole usually took several hours, large quantities of spaghetti often found their way into strange places, and Fray Bentos pies became the staple diet.

For the group, the welcome they received would be warm, and soon they would feel really at home as everyone sat around chatting, getting to know one another. They would be full of questions about *Memory*, what everything was and how she came to be there. Keith and the others soon warmed to their task of explaining the idiosyncrasies of living on board and were very soon sharing the wonderful story of how God had made it all possible.

Questions about *Memory* quickly turned into questions about God and somehow it was easy for even the shyest youngsters to talk about things that bothered them. Often it was very obvious that many young people thought that God was just for those who went to church and were prepared to obey lots of seemingly silly rules.

It was quite a revelation to hear how God worked in the lives of people like Keith and Gerry in a very down-to-earth way; that he was actually interested in each one of us and all our problems.

It was also a revelation for some of the youngsters to meet Christians who were full of fun and laughter and who obviously enjoyed themselves. As the talk turned to sailing next day, the groups became almost too excited to sleep.

At last the noisy chatter would die down and all would be quiet, except for the gentle creaking of *Memory* as she also settled for the night.

Next morning everyone would be up at the crack of dawn, as the temptation to go up on deck to see what was going on was too much. Sounds of breakfast preparation from the galley and the smell of bacon dragged the last sleeper from his bed.

After breakfast came a 'Thought for the Day' — something for everyone to chew over in their mind during the day — it might be just a song or a story.

There followed a mad scramble to get all the chores done — washing-up, peeling spuds, sweeping up — so that the serious business of the day could begin.

How much of the day was spent sailing depended on the tide. A tide morning and evening was ideal for a day out on the water, taking lunch and visiting some 'far away' place, such as Stone Point, or Mersea Island, or even Brightlingsea. The emphasis was always on being together, going somewhere together, in the assortment of dinghies and the motor-launch.

Back on board in the evening some of the group would rally round to help get a meal on the table, while others stowed the boats away, and did any other jobs which were needed. Often there would be a walk up the path to our sail-loft for fresh supplies of milk from the fridge, and any other requirements for the galley, and sometimes a quick visit to the shops for sweets.

After the meal, worn out by wind and sun, and beginning

31

to feel muscles that were complaining, people would be content to sit around and relive the day's experiences, or practise knots that had been needed during the day. And it was not long before the atmosphere became intimate and warm, and conversations begun on the previous evening were taken up again.

As time went by life on the barge got busier and busier, and groups began to ask about coming for weeks in the summer. It was a fresh milestone, and a great relief, to have the first resident Warden on board.

Graham, then a university student, was a dinghy sailor, but he needed more talents than this to look after the visiting group. By now the Fellowship had quite a collection of dinghies, including a couple of Wayfarers, a GP 14, a Mirror and a Duckling. There was also a work-boat, *Ada*, an ex-Admiralty cutter which was used as a safety boat. Graham's first lessons in handling *Ada* were eventful. As he rammed her into the side of *Memory* under Keith's watchful eye, he fully expected a blistering telling-off. But Keith was very patient. All he said was, 'You'll know next time!'

Being responsible for the group meant being aware of the rhythm of the tides and adapting to them — and not just when sailing. One night Graham and the group left the barge dry-shod for an evening out, only to find on their return that the tide had come in much more quickly than anticipated and they were stranded. There was no alternative. Graham had to whip off his jeans and wade to the barge for a dinghy to ferry everyone else across. This is not very easy in daylight, but at night it is almost impossible to see the path through the depth of water. A mistake results in a swim.

To be stranded on *Memory* was less frustrating than being stranded ashore, because at least there was easy access to a dinghy. It's possible then to row up the creek to the road, or even right up the road itself, when the tide comes up past the wooden yacht stores alongside the road. This event is a little startling for the unsuspecting car owner who leaves his car to go for a walk and becomes fascinated by the fact that the tide is in. On his return he may discover that his car has had a tidal wash. There have even been a couple of occasions when a car has been full to the roof.

The very high tides change the surroundings, so much so that one lad left alone on *Memory* while everyone was out sailing, went up on deck and panicked because he thought he was adrift in the middle of the Blackwater. It was a while before he realized that he was not actually moving and that there were some very comforting mooring chains to be seen.

Looking after the loos was high on the list of important tasks for the resident Warden. Those first primitive 'bucket and chuckit' type toilets were often a topic of conversation, particularly at meal-times. Visiting the loos on *Memory* was never a very private affair, and there was a rumour that someone once lasted for a whole week without using them. Little wonder that, when the council provided 'bright and shinies' a little way up the road, there were always those who would make a special pilgrimage twice a day.

There was also little encouragement to wash, as running water consisted of one cold-water tap two feet from the floor, which dripped continuously into a bucket. This was in fact a luxury, provided by water-tanks that had to be filled up by means of a collection of hoses joined together to reach all the way from the road to the barge. When the tanks were full, the unfortunate person delegated to turn off the supply at the road had to roll up his sleeve and plunge his arm as far as it would go into muddy, smelly water, in order to reach the stop-cock. This job was second only in unpleasantness to that of emptying the toilets.

In the early days anything biodegradable went over the side. The major concession with the loos was that the buckets were taken out into the estuary and emptied on a falling tide. It was important to remember which way the wind was blowing — and not to drop the bucket.

Living on board is an unusual experience for most people, and they therefore tend to accept easily the most unusual circumstances. One morning Graham woke to the sounds of paddling and, on going to investigate, discovered the resident group in pyjamas and wellies, splashing through six inches of water to get to the toilet. No one had thought that it might be wise to tell the Warden of this occurrence, because, if the tide was in, you had to expect such things! In fact the tide was out, and the bilge-pump had been switched off by mistake and for some odd reason had actually syphoned water back into the bilges. Three years later, when the same thing happened, people reacted in exactly the same manner, donning their boots and carrying on as if nothing was wrong.

Everything had to be organized around the sailing, which was, of course, governed by the tides. A very early tide could mean creeping out on the last of the tide on a misty morning with the sun just rising, and staying out for a whole day on the water. A later tide could mean just making it back to the barge at the end of the day, and sometimes having to push the dinghies through the mud for the last twenty feet. Graham would be blamed then for everyone being muddy, and it would be his responsibility to retrieve the fleet from further down the creek at midnight if the desire for a longer sail had meant leaving the boats there.

The creeks they explored were often new to Graham as well as to the group. Going up Old Hall, Salcott or round to Goldhanger would mean lunch sprawled out on grassy sea-walls; a day-trip to Brightlingsea or Stone Point, or a visit to Mersea, would mean a beach to play games on, or even a shop or a toilet to visit. Going across to Bradwell might well mean a walk around to St Peter's on the Wall, where St Cedd was supposed to have landed. It was a big responsibility for Graham to look after everyone while they were on the water, and his youth and inexperience kept him very dependent on God for protection and strength, and the many people interested in the barge who prayed for him.

Sometimes a boat would capsize in a sudden gust of wind, or because someone did something silly, but always, thankfully, everyone was safely rescued. In order that youngsters should be familiar with capsize drill, every sailing course would see a Wayfarer turned over off the end of the pontoons. Graham had this down to a fine art, and would clamber out onto the centre-board, right the boat and clamber back in, only ever getting wet up to the knees. This was too much for one of his crew who had been on the wet end of the capsize and, on bailing the boat out, George aimed his bucket of water expertly at Graham.

Each group was different. Most people were fairly casual and, if they went to church, were likely to appear in wellies and fisherman's smocks. Not so one group, who insisted on dresses and suits. They walked across the muddy marsh as if they were in the high street. One particular group from Devon were really kitted out for every occasion, and produced long dresses and party gear in order to go out for dinner to celebrate a birthday. In the end they celebrated an engagement as well and, what with washing every day in hot water, set some all-time records for the barge.

The atmosphere on board was always infectious and one lad, who came down having found us through the yellow pages in the phone-book, was obviously very affected by what the barge stood for. This came out clearly in his remonstration with someone sharing his cabin:

'Look here, mate. I don't want to be unchristian, but will you stop b____ing about?'

The end to the week was usually a barbecue, which meant a trek around the sea-wall to collect driftwood, which would be loaded up into dinghies and brought back to make a fire near the old sailing club hut. Food cooked down below tasted better out of doors and a sing-song around the bonfire would extend well into the night. However late they were to bed, there would nearly always be some who would cram into the master's cabin to pray together and praise God for his goodness at the end of each day.

Relationships grew and blossomed. For all his busyness, Graham found time for courtship. Mandy was also on board, often busy in the galley, and sharing the day's activities. They would see each other after a hard day's work, exhausted, under pressure from people and things, and first thing in the morning when they had not had enough sleep. They must have been good times though, for they decided to get married, even though Mandy could cook for twenty-two but not for two, and despite knowing the worst about each other. Theirs was the first of many courtships on *Memory*.

4

Turning-point

The second summer Graham and Mandy spent on board, they felt like old hands. But Graham found it particularly difficult to cope with the maintenance problems which were always cropping up. So, when David joined the two of them for the summer, things really began to look up, because he knew how to make things with wood.

David's coming heralded a great era of improvement: skylights stopped leaking, the sliding hatch was replaced, decks were caulked and, most wonderful of all, a sturdy gang-plank complete with hand-rail appeared. This was an unheard-of luxury. No more would there be screams from all the girls who came on board, convinced they were going to fall into the mud.

David was not really a newcomer to *Memory*. He had been coming down to Tollesbury since he was thirteen years old, working first on the smack and then on the barge. The opportunity to be on *Memory* for a whole summer was too good to be true.

It marked a turning-point in David's life and that of Fellowship Afloat. He had only intended it to be a diversion between college and going abroad on Voluntary Service Overseas but very soon life on board, and the surroundings and the people he met, made David begin to feel that he never wanted to leave Tollesbury. It was hard to think about cholera and typhoid injections in preparation for life in Kenya.

His growing friendship with Tim, who lived in the village, and Iain, whose father ran the village shop, seemed much more real and important. Of the many people who regularly helped on the barge, with cooking, sailing, maintenance and whatever, these two were perhaps the most faithful. Through them David began to get to know the village; and the village people began to get to know him.

By the end of August Graham and Mandy had left, and fewer people came down to the barge. Then David began fully to appreciate his friendship with Iain and his family, and the welcome he found in the home above the shop. Iain loved to be on the barge and appreciated his acceptance there. David for his part did not need much persuading when Iain said, 'Come home for a meal?'

He needed even less when Iain's mum said, 'Stay the night. It's much too cold on the barge.'

After one of David's visits to the shop, Iain nearly choked with laughter as he heard a woman say:

'He looks a shady character. Lives out on the marshes, doesn't he? Some rum people down there!'

He wondered what his father's reply would be.

'Oh, he's all right,' replied Colin. 'We know him quite well; he came to dinner last night.'

The woman's face was a picture as she tried to take in this piece of information.

'Well, he does look scruffy, and you never know these days!' The lady stomped off with her purchases.

'There's never a dull moment in this shop,' said Colin to Iain. 'I bet David will laugh when he hears that.'

On one occasion David was extra-grateful he had spent the night with the family: he needed an alibi when he came under suspicion because of his white wellies.

The muddy path to *Memory* meant that boots were always needed. If he was going into the village David would leave his wellies in the yacht stores that the Fellowship rented. This was the bottom floor of one of the stores, and very important to the work on *Memory*, because it provided storage space plus somewhere to work on boats. It was also a very convenient place to leave things. The door was often left open, so when the local police spotted David's boots sitting there, they got quite excited. The night before, the chemist's shop in the village had been burgled, and the main clue was a set of boot-prints all over the floor. On closer investigation they discovered that David's boots fitted those prints exactly.

When David sauntered back down the road and came to collect his boots, he was greeted by two policemen, one of whom said:

'Excuse me, sir. These your boots, are they?'

'Yes, they are,' said David, looking mystified.

'I see, and where do you live?'

'Out on *Memory*, on the saltings.'

'There last night, were you?'

'No, I was in the village.'

'In the village, eh? What were you doing there?'

'Visiting friends.'

'What time did you leave?'

'Oh, I've only just left — I stayed the night.'

'Well, I think we'd better go and visit your friends. Who are they?'

'The folk at the shop.'

'Oh yes. Well, perhaps we've been jumping to conclusions.'

So David was taken in the police car to see if his story would be corroborated. Of course it was, and there were apologies all round, and much laughter over the thought that David was nearly arrested because of his wellie boots.

Apart from the need for a good character reference, David really needed his retreat up the hill when things got lonesome on the barge. It was good to be able to spend some evenings sitting in front of the fire, and sleeping in a bed that was going to stay dry, even if it rained. So, when his spartan existence became too much, Iain would drag him away from the barge.

Another important friendship was with Tony, who owned *Galliard*, a beautiful thirty-foot sailing cruiser which he had built himself and now kept on the saltings in a mud-berth not far from *Memory*. He often came on board at weekends. Tony also appreciated this particular area of saltings, where the scene changes with the tide. Every time he drove over the humpy-backed bridge, which was part of the sea-wall, and saw once more the four Edwardian yacht stores, which stood with their backs to the estuary and enticed him to leave his car as soon as possible to walk beyond them out onto the marsh, he could feel the excitement welling up. Soon he would be on the barge looking across to Mersea Island and watching the tide come up the creek.

Betty, his wife, often came with him. David looked forward to their visits and occasionally went out on *Galliard*.

One particular mid-week evening found David and Iain out on *Galliard* in the fog with Tony and Keith's brother, Stuart.

'There's Bradwell lights,' said Iain decisively.

'That's not Bradwell,' scoffed Stuart. 'How can that possibly be Bradwell?'

'Of course it is,' said Iain. 'Look, pal, how many times have I sailed into this creek? That's Bradwell! We bear round here, Tony.'

'You'd better be right,' said Tony as he swung the helm of *Galliard*. 'I'll be glad to be back on the mooring. This fog makes you feel you could be anywhere.'

Seconds later, the boat lurched and came to a standstill.

'We're aground,' said Stuart. 'I told you that wasn't Bradwell. We're on Cocum Hills.'

'Well, it is a bit shallow for South Channel, I'll grant you that,' said Iain sheepishly.

'What's going on?' enquired David, popping up from below, where he had been brewing tea.

Tony was throwing the engine into reverse, and Stuart and Iain had leapt onto the stern deck and were bouncing up and down, but the tide was ebbing fast, and they were well and truly stuck.

'So much for your navigation,' said Tony to Iain. 'Maybe it would be a good idea to use a compass next time.'

Sailing home in the dark and the fog and not using a compass did seem a bit lunatic, but Iain had been very convincing about where they were, and land had not been very far away. Had the rest of the crew known then that Iain was one day destined to be a navigator on a submarine, they might have had even more comment to make. It would take a long time for Iain to live this down.

'Now what?' asked David. 'We'll be here till morning!'

'Well, we need to phone home,' said Tony. 'Betty won't be very pleased.'

'Neither will Anne,' said Stuart. 'She'll wonder what on earth's happened to us.'

'Well, we can take the dinghy ashore,' said Iain. 'We must be able to find a phone.'

So David and Iain went off in the dinghy, hoping there would be enough water to get ashore, while Stuart and Tony tried to sort out the boat.

The previous weekend, Tony and Betty had had a lovely sail on the Saturday, ending up in the Pyefleet, where they found the smack *William Emily* with three or four people on board. They had a really pleasant evening together and looked forward to sailing back in company the next day. However, the next day it blew up quite rough and Tony did not feel too confident about bringing *Galliard* back with just Betty as crew. The smack did not have a large enough crew to split, so it seemed that the best thing to do was to leave *Galliard* in the Pyefleet and all sail back together in the smack. Tony would be able to muster some help to fetch *Galliard* during the week.

Stuart, Iain and David had been only too happy to help. So, earlier that evening, they had put a dinghy on the roof of the land-rover, driven over, launched the dinghy and rowed out to *Galliard*. If they had been wiser, they would probably have delayed the exercise in view of the mist that was coming down, but Tony was anxious to have *Galliard* back in Tollesbury. Now he was wishing that he had been a little more patient.

'I reckon this fog is going to get thicker,' said Tony.

'No!' said Stuart. 'It'll all be gone in the morning. What time's the tide? When will we float?'

'About an hour before high water, I s'pose,' said Tony. 'What's that, about six to half past?'

'I reckon!' said Stuart. 'I wonder how long those two will be? Young Iain's an idiot! And we're bigger ones for being convinced by him.'

'I'll put the kettle on,' said Tony. 'Gosh, I'm a bit peckish. No supper at "The Hope" tonight! I'll bet there's nothing to eat on board!'

He went down below and started to rummage in the cupboards.

'There's some bread that's OK,' came the triumphant shout. 'There must be some soup somewhere, and here's some mousetrap cheese.'

'Great!' said Stuart. At the thought of food he soon cheered up, so when the others arrived back they settled down to quite a feast.

'When are you off to foreign parts then, David?' asked Stuart.

'You don't want to go off to Africa!' said Tony. 'You never know what might happen to you. Much better to stay in Tollesbury.'

David smiled. The summer on board *Memory* had made him feel that he belonged. He was due to go out with Voluntary Service Overseas at Christmas, and it looked as if he would be going to Kenya, although he was still waiting for confirmation.

'I suppose it will be January,' he said. 'I should be getting a letter from them any time.'

'There's enough voluntary service to be done on the barge without going abroad, I should have thought,' said Tony. 'Seriously, David, why don't you stay? I know there are enormous needs abroad, but you're just the person we need on board *Memory*. Look at all the practical things that need doing. If you were there all through the winter, it would make such a difference.'

'You ought to stay,' agreed Iain.

'I feel I've committed myself to VSO now,' said David, slowly.

'But you'd rather be here, really,' stated Iain.

'Well, I guess I would in many ways,' said David. 'Going to Kenya's a bit unknown and I certainly enjoy being here. But it's not just a question of which I'd rather do. I want to be sure I'm in the right place. Of course, they may not have a placement for me,' he added thoughtfully.

'We need someone with skill and who knows what needs doing,' Stuart said. 'That's you, David. You know just what you're letting yourself in for if you stay with us. And you know how you love the barge.'

'What do you think Keith would say?'

'He'd be over the moon, you know he would. Think of all the worry it would take from him. Someone to get the dinghies ready, look after the barge. We need a full-time Warden, a bit of continuity, someone who's here all the time and not just in the summer months.'

'It would be good to have the barge open throughout the winter,' said Tony. He grinned, 'Besides, I could come and stay, then!'

They talked well into the night, and by the time they went to bed, David was finally convinced that he should talk things over with Keith and let VSO know the position.

Afterwards, David always said it was a deliberate ploy of Iain's to strand them on the mud and persuade him to stay in Tollesbury.

When the alarm went off next morning, Stuart poked his head through the hatch to see if the mist had gone.

'Crumbs! You can't see anything this morning. It's a real pea-souper.'

'Well, we must get back,' insisted Tony. 'I'll have to get into work by this afternoon.'

'If Iain uses a compass this time, we might manage it!' suggested Stuart.

'OK! OK!' said Iain. 'Come on, let's get going, the boat's nearly afloat.'

'Stop nattering then, and get the kettle on,' said Tony.

Soon they were creeping through the fog under engine and praying that there would be no one else stupid enough to be out in the fog too, because they did not fancy having to avoid something which suddenly appeared out of the gloom — if it did not hit them first.

At last there was a shout from David, who was sitting on the foredeck, peering out into the swirling fog.

'There's the Nass. We've found it.'

The Nass Beacon marked the end of the spit that jutted

out from Shingle Hills, and was very important to sailors finding their way into South Channel.

'Due west then, I reckon,' said Iain. 'We'll have to guess when to turn in.'

After a short while, with everyone peering into the gloom and seeing nothing, Iain said, 'Change course now to 225°. That should do it.'

Any time now they should see a buoy or a withy, marking the channel, or even some mud.

Tony said, 'Surely we should be in the channel by now?'

The entrance to South Channel is tricky, even with good visibility. At low tide, it's possible to see the spit that curves half-way across the channel, so the withies must be followed very carefully. Many a sailor has spent a day on the mud here because he has misjudged it.

Now Tony became suspicious that they were not in the channel at all. The echo-sounder told them that they were in very deep water, and they could only conclude that somehow they must have crossed over Shingle Hills.

'We're back in the Blackwater,' said Tony. 'I don't think navigating's your thing, Iain!'

They had no idea where they were, or what direction to go in, so it was difficult to know whether to let down the anchor, or to go on and risk crashing into something, or perhaps going aground again.

Then Tony came up with a bright idea. He switched off the engine and listened in the quietness.

'There, you can hear Bradwell power station,' he said. 'It's over there. All we have to do is creep north north-east until the echo-sounder says it's shallow, edge along Shingle Hills, and then cross over them.'

'Good thinking!' said Stuart. 'But it would be good to have a bit more idea of where we are.'

'Let's all take a bearing on the sound of Bradwell, then, and take the average,' suggested Tony. 'That can't be far out.'

So that is what they did. If Bradwell power station had annoyed them in the past, with its continuous hum, it was a blessing now, and by stopping every now and then and taking more bearings and watching the echo-sounder, they found Shingle Hills, edged along until they judged they could cross over (the tide was still making, so even if they went aground they would soon float off) and then crept down the other side. Eventually they spotted the buoys and even the withies became visible, and before long they were into the Fleet, keeping a careful look-out to avoid moored boats. What a relief it was to pick up *Galliard*'s mooring and know that very soon they would be back on board the barge.

It had been quite a journey, and it marked a quite momentous decision in David's life. A visit to Keith settled that he should 'winter on the barge' and give up his thoughts of going to Kenya. It was a decision that he never regretted, or felt to be wrong, and one that was to have far-reaching effects on *Memory*. She now became someone's home.

5

A Romantic Winter

I was thrilled when David rang to say that he was staying in Tollesbury. I had known him for a couple of years, and he had introduced me to the joys of a camping holiday and life on the barge.

As his plan to go abroad became more definite, I had become more and more aware of the gap there would be in my life if David no longer popped round to my flat for coffee, or to see what he could cook in my kitchen. This was quite an admission, if only to myself, because only a few months earlier Stuart, whom I knew quite well, had said to me:

'It's time you got yourself a man, Mags!'

'Well, none seem to come my way — besides, I'm busy,' was my reply.

'What about David — just the guy for you.'

'You're joking!' I said. 'He's much too young for me.'

'You'll eat your words — you'll see,' laughed Stuart.

'No chance!' I was very sure of myself.

However, I was not at all sure now, because David did not really seem younger than me; in fact he seemed older. I sometimes thought he must have been born old and wise. We seemed to share so many interests and now here I was sharing David's excitement about being full-time Warden on the barge and making *Memory* his home.

I had been down to the barge two or three times and could not make up my mind whether it was the barge I enjoyed visiting, or David. I really did not know what to make of our friendship. Neither, it seemed, did anyone else.

It was at this point that I really began to get to know Keith and Gerry, and their two girls, Anna (then five) and Clare (three). It was obvious that they were as pleased as I was that David was now looking after the barge on a full-time basis. It must have been quite a relief to know they need not journey to Tollesbury quite as often. Now there was no fear that someone would go down one day in the winter and find that the barge had sunk.

So, on many weekends, I would leave all the comforts of my flat, drive the forty-odd miles to Tollesbury, and join in the challenge for survival on the barge through the winter.

Keeping warm and dry was the biggest problem. Not for David the luxury of a delivery of coal. Fuel for the fire meant a trip collecting driftwood, and an hour on deck chopping it down to a reasonable size. On many weekends a few people would come down to make up a working party, and this was one of the major tasks.

It amazed me that people seemed happy to put up with all manner of discomforts on the barge and to spend hour after hour working hard, sometimes in the wet and cold, and on not very pleasant tasks. No one seemed to mind sitting at the table with water dripping into their cornflakes, or their left ear, or, worse still, waking up to a wet sleeping-bag. Washing in cold water, sitting in a draught, no television, no lights in the cabins, breaking the ice on the water-tanks to get a cup of tea (even putting ice in the porridge), the scent of Elsan fluid in the nostrils — all these seemed part of the charm of wintering on the saltings.

When I first went down to the barge, the path always seemed to be muddy, and I had a hard time convincing David that I really did not mind, because I had been brought up in wellie boots. However, there came a day when you could walk down the path in your carpet slippers in January. This was the result of several concentrated efforts which began with a shramming party.

As this always seems to be a winter occupation — there is never time in the summer — it is always bitterly cold. The one and only shramming party I went on was memorable. We took our old launch, *Ada*, and a lighter, lots of large plastic

46

bags and shovels and set off on the last of the tide. Arriving on Shingle Hills, we beached *Ada*, and set to work filling the sacks with the shram that would transform our path. You would think that this would be a pretty warm occupation, but we were all fairly frozen. When we had loaded the lighter with all we thought she could take without sinking, it was lunch-time — time to brew up hot soup on the gas burner, eat sandwiches and, surprise of surprises, David had packed fresh cream cakes for us all. He must have known we would be in need of a psychological boost.

Since we had been so energetic, there was no more shram digging to do, but we would have to wait nearly two hours for the tide to refloat us. Most people opted to huddle in the cuddy of *Ada*, but John, Tim, David and I decided to walk along the 'hills' towards the Nass. In fact we had never realized just how far the tide went out and how near we could get to the Nass Beacon. We felt we could almost wade out to it. But even more fascinating was the miniature landscape in the mud — it formed cliffs, and walking on them we felt like giants walking along a cliff-top coastline. We found the remains of ancient fish-traps and saw a great deal of bird-life: flocks of dunlin and sanderling, a pair of oyster-catchers strutting about like proud peacocks and very distinctive with their bright orange beaks, the familiar Brent geese and even cormorants. It was as if they were all giants too, and each ripple in the mud, or gulley carved out by the tide, was transformed into a make-believe world.

Looking across to Bradwell, the beach looked almost inviting, but we were so close to the power station that it lost its usual look of mystery and just loomed, big and ugly. The river was empty. It would have been nice to have sailed across and visited St Peter's on the Wall, but we would leave that for a warm summer's day.

On our return to *Ada* we were greeted by glum, cold people who were sorry they had not joined us in our walk. However, a cup of tea, and then we could all spring into action. The tide would soon have us afloat. We were glad we had taken the precaution of bringing a water-pump, because the lighter leaked quite badly, and, with its extra load, the

The Hard, Tollesbury.

pump needed to work full pelt all the way back to *Memory*. It was a relief to arrive back safely. We would not have been pleased if all the shram had ended up on the mud at the bottom of the creek.

The next task was to unload the sacks and use the wheelbarrows to get them to the places where the path was worst. Gradually, we have changed the path from being a quagmire for most of the year (for even in summer the high tides would soon make it muddy) to being reasonably firm and only a bit sticky in very wet weather. Once or twice we have felt able to spend money on hogging, but for the most part we have relied simply on the hard work of many volunteers.

From the very beginning we have been grateful for work parties when all sorts of tasks can be achieved in the minimum amount of time. Sometimes it has been just a day visit to carry out a giant spring-clean at the beginning of the season. On one occasion we sanded and varnished the massive kelson which is *Memory*'s backbone. It was no easy task, as this giant timber, once a whole tree, runs the length of the barge and is pitted and scratched by age. Black-varnishing the outside of the barge is an annual task for which we always welcome help.

On other occasions, when just one or two people are struggling to complete a major project, such as refitting the loos or the galley, maintenance seems a long, hard haul.

During David's first winter, one of his main concerns was to cure some of the leaks, beginning with the ones above his bunk! A long, dry spell can lull you into a sense of security and if it does not rain you do not know where the leaks are anyway. When it did rain, David got quite excited and prepared to go round with a notebook and even mark all the leaks. However, the long, dry spell had dried everything out, so that now the whole boat leaked like a sieve. Perhaps it would be more expedient to wait until everything 'took up' a bit and then tackle the persistent leaks.

The sheer enormity of the tasks required to improve 'home comforts' led David to adopt a very optimistic, positive approach.

If someone complained of a leak he would say: 'That's not a leak — that's condensation.'

If someone complained of the cold he would say: 'Nonsense, it's not cold — just look at this lovely fire.'

And if someone complained about the mud he would say: 'It's only mud — it won't hurt you.'

This approach must have kept him sane, and gave visitors the feeling that it was quite a privilege to experience life on *Memory*.

Passing his driving test and buying a mini for £5 made quite a difference to David. This ancient mini had a lot of character. The driver's door had a tendency to fall off, there was a button on the floor to start the engine, and the speedometer needle whooshed into the petrol gauge when it passed fifty miles an hour, causing one passenger to get very excited and think he was doing 100. The sight of the road rushing past through the holes in the floor made it feel like 150! The fact that David was always late increased this feeling, and Tony always clutched his prayer-book when travelling with him.

The petrol gauge did not work either, and David carried a stick of iroko in the back to keep a check on levels. A skid into a local ditch meant that a new bonnet was needed. A 'fibreglass job' was fitted with a hinge at the front and fastened at the back with what were hardly more than rubber bands. On pulling up outside the 'Red Lion' in D'Arcy one day, the bonnet shot forward with a loud crash, smashing the headlights and causing the inmates of the pub to rush out to see what was happening.

The local bus service came to a halt at seven o'clock, which did not do much for a social life. Now David could visit Keith and Gerry in Witham and Stuart and Anne in Totham much more easily. He could also visit me, though the demands of the barge were such that he did not do this very often. Usually, it was I who drove down to Tollesbury for the weekend, to share in whatever was going on.

Winter evenings round the fire, pretending not to notice the howling draught; knot-practising sessions, where we made mats and tied Turk's heads round Tony's boat-hook; toast and hot chocolate at midnight; and waking up in the morning to see your breath and hear strains of *Messiah* (difficult to recognize from Tony's rendering) — all these became a way of life. Tony, true to his promise, would often be down at weekends, working on *Galliard* and enjoying our company on the barge. Sometimes he would decide on a bit of *cordon bleu* cooking. *Coq au vin* has never tasted so good since.

After a good meal, extending to cheese and biscuits and

real coffee kept hot on the fire, we would dream about all the alterations we could make to the barge. The saloon was to be completely redesigned, with tables that were raised on pulleys to the deckhead so that, when there was no group on board, easy chairs would be miraculously pulled out from some hidden corner (where, I cannot imagine), so that we could all sit comfortably around the fire.

There would be a kind of wheel-house built on deck, so that wet gear and wellies would not have to come down below, giving more space in the fo'c'sle. We would have separate loos for ladies and gents, with hot showers heated by some solar system — the favourite one was a coiled black hosepipe on deck.

A visit to a store in a nearby village stocked with army and navy surplus goods was an education. You could buy anything from a pencil lead to a dumper truck, and of course they were all bargains! Anything you asked for they had, unless it had been sold the previous week. They once had a run on fire-engines, and there was a wonderful space-suit hanging up for months.

We always seemed to go there when it was bitterly cold. It was possible to stand in front of a great, roaring red-hot blow-heater and still be cold in their huge warehouse. When we could drag ourselves away from the heat, there were wellies and jumpers, waterproofs and all manner of tools to look at — the list was endless. And they were all in racks about twenty feet high.

On one visit we bought a wonderful set of green waterproofs for visitors to the barge. We were delighted with our purchase, but I doubt if any of those who wore them were so appreciative. Every suit was massive. They must have been made for men over six foot tall. Rolling up the legs was of little use, because the crutch came down below the knees, severely hampering any activity more strenuous than a slow waddle. How people sailed in them I'll never know, and they certainly did not keep the wet out. They became known as 'gumby' suits because everyone looked such an idiot wearing one.

Of course it was not always cold and wet on the barge and,

as spring came and the boats went back in the water and groups started to arrive, those winter evenings became a memory, and the barge was alive with young people once more. What a contrast it was and how good to share in the excitement of a group as they experienced things for the first time.

Even so, I often felt this was not much of a way to conduct a courtship, for David's first responsibility was to the group, and although I came and helped in the galley on many weekends, I sometimes felt a bit jealous of the demands everyone made on his time. Gradually, though, I came to love the barge, and being with all the different groups as much as David did. I enjoyed being part of all the activities and sharing in the love and fellowship which always seemed to be present.

6

Doggy Interlude

From the very beginning of our relationship, it was quite plain to me that if I married David I would be marrying Fellowship Afloat as well. He was so immersed in the whole world of the salt-marsh, boats, sailing, and most of all the people who were regularly involved, or who visited, and the vision for sharing things with them. In a way this was how I found myself sailing up the Thames with him on the smack. I seemed to be irresistibly drawn to the life of the barge, as well as to David. Our trip on *Odd Times* had served to show me this.

To spend time with David was to share the excitement of the first glimpse of each salt-marsh plant as it appeared; his love of *Memory* and interest in her history; the welcome he gave to everyone who came on board. Walking round the sea-wall he would talk about reclaimed land and the remains of the creeks. He would show me a red hill, a relic of Roman times when they burnt fires to evaporate the sea water to leave salt. I would learn the names of the different birds, spotting a heron if I was lucky.

David always seemed to know everyone and something interesting about them, and he also knew all about traditional boats, what they were made of, the best way to mend them, and the delightful names (such as baggy wrinkle and tholpins) by which everything was known.

As well as all this he was an expert cook and instinctively knew what went best with what. He had introduced pastry-making to the barge and endless culinary delights, including

53

barge pizza. Like the other volunteer cooks, I was often very frightened of him in the galley, when he peered under the saucepan-lids, in case I did anything wrong.

Not many people are given a puppy instead of an engagement ring. But Periwinkle was David's present to me, though she lived with him on the barge until we were married. The name had to be one of a list of flowers, none of which seemed very appropriate. But a periwinkle is a shellfish as well as a flower and so we thought that the name had a nice, nautical flavour.

Most of the time she was called Peri, and although I only saw her every two or three weeks, usually on the barge, I remember her vividly as a puppy, getting into all sorts of trouble. For two or three weeks she was confined to the barge, which was very trying for everyone. Puddles and heaps are not pleasant, even when they are only a puppy's, and it must have been very unhygienic.

'Out of the galley!' was probably the first real command Peri learned. But at six o'clock in the morning, before anyone except me was awake, she would sneak out of the master's cabin, where she slept in a box under the table, and run along the corridor to the galley, where she would pull over the rubbish-bin and rummage through the contents.

One morning she had a real bonus. She found a cupboard open and was able to demolish half a pound of butter before anyone found her. She was lucky to find butter on the barge!

After her morning sortie in the galley she would return along the corridor and find her way into people's cabins. She was small enough to get under the gap at the bottom of the door. More cunningly, she actually managed to get under the corridor from the toilet area and would then pop out from under some unsuspecting sleeper's bed. One poor man had a real fright. He woke expecting to see his wife's face and instead had the wet nose of a black puppy thrust onto his pillow.

These little journeys under the corridor had to end when David discovered that Peri was leaving little 'parcels' behind, and so he blocked up all the entrances.

As soon as Peri heard signs of life in the master's cabin

she would go back to investigate. Tony often shared the cabin with David at weekends, and his cries could be heard the full length of the barge.

'Get off, dog. Let me get my trousers on!'

'I hate dogs — they should not be allowed on boats!'

'Come back with my socks, you horrid beast!'

Peri often had cornflakes for breakfast, and somehow her ears would always end up in the milk. One morning, to her delight, she found a face very close to hers. Someone had decided to sleep on the kelson — not a very comfortable berth, and it was surprising he was still asleep. A small tongue and wet ears soon roused him from his slumbers.

Peri really was very much David's dog and went everywhere with him. She was also very much a part of barge life, and being a flat-coated retriever with a very individual character, she always attracted attention, if only to ask what make she was.

Although not everyone recognized her breeding, she left no one in any doubt as to how she was to be treated. She often gave the appearance of being rather snooty. When everyone was seated in the saloon for a meal or a meeting, she would sit up in the corridor and survey us down the length of her nose. However, this did not mean she was unfriendly. In fact at times she was much too friendly, especially if she met some stranger on the path. Two large, muddy paws on clean clothes were not popular.

The youngsters who came on board loved Peri and spent hours playing with her. There was always someone who would make a special fuss of her — and often someone feeling a bit homesick, whom Peri helped to settle in.

Her real puppy days were over by the time we got married and she came to live in our new flat. Since Christmas was a very quiet time on the barge, it seemed a good opportunity to get married. We spent a week on the Isle of Wight, without Peri, where we managed to see plenty of boats and visit another sailing centre, just so as not to suffer withdrawal symptoms.

Peri was very excited to see us on our return and, when we went to bed, approved of the new rule of everyone together.

With an enormous stag-like jump she landed in between us.

She soon adapted to flat life, but spent as much time as ever on the marshes with David. I played a very unimportant part in her life. She was still very much David's dog until she was about eighteen months old.

Then one day when I patted her, she seemed to rattle! In fact she sounded just like a bag of stones. David said I was imagining things, and actually picked her up and shook her. He put the noise in her tummy down to water.

However, the next day the rattle became unmistakable. When she shook we could hear it — even when she wagged her tail; and when she sat down, it went clink-clunk.

I was not quite sure what reaction I would get when I walked into the vet's surgery and said, 'My dog rattles!' But I need not have worried. They had met this problem before.

'She's probably swallowed some stones,' said the vet. 'I once had an Alsatian rattle in here with seventy-six stones in his tummy.'

'Oh dear!' I said. 'What does that mean?'

'It means an operation, I'm afraid,' the vet replied. 'Or very soon they will cut off her food supply, because eventually they will go down further than her stomach and get stuck!'

With this he got out his stethoscope to listen to the stones, and was unable to hear anything. I felt rather stupid and began to think that I really was imagining it. However, he was fairly convinced by what I had told him previously and said,

'It's a bit odd, but maybe they've settled. We'll give her an x-ray to make sure. That needs a general anaesthetic so, if there's anything there, we'll carry on and operate.'

I was really scared and shaky when I delivered a very bouncy and excited dog to the surgery at the appointed time.

'You won't bounce like that this evening,' laughed the receptionist, as Peri trotted off down the corridor with her.

She had ten stones in her tummy.

I went to pick her up, a matter of hours after what was quite a major operation, and she actually walked along to me. It was a bit of a plod, her head was right down, but she managed just one wag of her tail by way of greeting. When she arrived home, she bravely tackled the stairs, but would not settle down anywhere, although her bed was put near the fire. Eventually it became clear, after she had wandered painfully round the flat and then just stood pathetically near the settee, that that was where she wanted to go. It was more than I could do to refuse. So that was the end of the rule that said, 'No dogs on the furniture.'

Apart from when I coaxed her to go outside, that is where she stayed to convalesce. With great difficulty the settee would be carried into our bedroom at night, so that we would hear her if she started to lick the stitches. I could not bear the thought of putting a bucket on her head to stop her doing this, so it was fortunate that it was the Easter holidays and I was able to spend time with her.

We had a group on board and they all came to visit Peri. The way she lay on the settee and received everyone was very funny. Swallowing stones was something of a novelty, and she created quite a bit of interest, as well as sympathy.

Because I spent so much time with Periwinkle, our relationship changed. Previously she had paid me little attention. But now each seemed to know what the other was thinking. She anticipated my every move, and I always knew what she wanted. Now, if she was with both of us and we went separate ways she was in real confusion. Before she would have followed David without hesitation.

Because she was always with one of us, I was surprised to find her sitting on the doorstep one morning. She had gone down to the barge for breakfast with David, but he was not due back yet, and anyway there was no sign of him, only the dog. In she came, nose sniffing, for my parents were staying with us and my father was enjoying some bacon — Peri's favourite. I had a feeling that David did not know that Peri was no longer with him, so I gave the barge a ring and, sure enough, he thought she was still on board.

'She's just presented herself at the door — I think she fancies sharing Dad's breakfast!'

There was a chuckle at the other end of the line.

'That's probably right. We had scrambled egg for

breakfast and there wasn't any left over. She did look a bit put out when there was none for her.'

What a naughty dog — but she got her bacon-rinds!

Periwinkle just loved the water. She loved to splash around in it, shake it over everyone, swim in it, bury her nose in it and she never tired of fetching sticks out of it. If she was on the barge, as soon as the tide started to lap against the pier she would be up on deck and down the gang-plank. Sometimes she would sit at the end of the gang-plank and cry for permission, but this was really only a formality. She was the most tireless of playmates and her energy even outlasted the youngsters'.

When we had a group of more difficult youngsters on board, it was often hard work keeping them occupied and out of mischief, and the helpers were always exhausted before the youngsters showed the least sign of being tired. But Peri was never tired of playing and, as splashing about in the water and paddling around in the mud were favourite occupations of many of the youngsters, she was very popular.

She was not so popular with those of us who had to deal with muddy, wet people and dogs afterwards, but she was a great asset as we tried to communicate and help these youngsters to appreciate the barge and all we had to offer. Sometimes we would have a youngster on board who was shy, or who did not really want to come, or who found it difficult to feel at home and join in with things. Then, of course, Peri would be invaluable, because she always expected to be everyone's friend and made a fuss of people.

Sometimes it would be possible to have a conversation like this through the dog with a youngster who would not talk person to person. Having a dog on board is a bit like having a small child. However big and brave you may have to appear before other people, you can be soft and silly with a dog. Peri was often a means of breaking down the barriers. Then the real person behind the hard shell would begin to emerge.

Peri was by no means the only dog who came on board.

We grew so used to having them around that we did not really notice, even if they caused a major disruption. We were used to taking things in our stride and always being flexible, and often did not realize how strange things must have seemed to visitors who were not used to our ways. We accepted the disruptions caused by small children in much the same way. That was really what the barge was all about. Everyone was welcome, and we were always particularly anxious to make families feel wanted.

On one occasion we were holding a serious meeting in the saloon with a visiting speaker, Graham Leavers, when Peri and two other dogs came charging down below with a great deal of noise, rushed through the saloon and slid to a halt in the galley. No one batted an eyelid except poor Graham, who could not make out what was happening. We learned later that he felt that he had failed, for it seemed as if everyone was much more interested in all the dogs than in what he was saying. In fact, everyone appreciated his visit very much. It was the beginning of our association with the youth organization called The Frontier Youth Trust for which he worked, and of our friendship with Graham, which we valued greatly. He had a great deal of experience with difficult youngsters in a coffee-bar that he ran, and through his extended family, which never seemed able to turn people away. Graham and his wife Twink were a great encouragement to us and an example of the commitment required to reach the more difficult youngsters whom we entertained on board.

I was often accused of treating Peri like a person, but I never went as far as one of our visitors, who attributed to her powers that even I would not have dared to do. I would often get so involved in the galley that I would forget that Peri was even around. Anyway, if she was not down below, and the tide was in, it was a safe bet that she would be playing in the water. One Sunday morning I suddenly remembered her and went up on deck to check that she was all right, and found her splashing about and biting the clagweed that always seem to float near the edge of the water.

I had a fright when a voice came from the stern deck. I had not realized that anyone was on board and the words made my heart miss a beat.

'Your dog swam across the creek and back, you know.'

'Surely she didn't!' I exclaimed. 'Just now? But the creek's so busy!'

Even as I spoke, three cruisers made their way to the marina, as one made its way out. It was quite a long way to the far side of the creek, and very dangerous. I could not believe that Peri really had swum across.

'Don't worry. She looked both ways first.'

'Now I know you're joking,' I said.

'No, really, I'm not joking. She swam across to have a game with a dalmatian who was playing with a stick. She's quite clever, your dog, you know.'

I found it hard to believe that she had coped intelligently with the river traffic, since she had no road sense at all. I once went home to find her sitting on the settee, obviously in a state of shock. On asking David what was the matter with her, he said that she had gone under a car as it came over the humpy-backed bridge. She certainly had no idea about traffic on the road.

It was always fun to take Peri out with us. She was good in the car and would stay there happily, if need be, and she was always interested in new places. Her fascination with the water was usually a major feature. In Tollesbury the tide creeps in and out slowly, and the first time she met the sea that 'comes at you', she went absolutely mad. You could almost see the disbelief on her face, and then the pure enjoyment as she scampered about, every so often getting swamped.

Sadly there came a day when Peri was no longer able to visit the barge because she found it so painful to get around. She had cancer and, at less than eight years, we felt a little cheated. However, she was a noble lady, and left us with a great many happy and funny memories.

About a week before we had to say goodbye, she managed to walk a little way down the path when the tide was in and have a last paddle. She even had a last bite at the clagweed, and had a good sniff of the sea that she used to be able to smell, even from the flat, where she would jump up at the window and ask to be allowed out for a swim. When she had gone, we were not the only ones to miss her.

7

Damaged Lives

It was easy to take for granted what was really something very special. The atmosphere of *Memory* was unique. Her position, stuck out in the middle of a salt-marsh, made quite an impact on those who came to stay. And the caring community of volunteers and full-time workers who welcomed everyone to share in life on board were difficult things to explain to people who had not been to see for themselves.

As we began to extend the welcome to youngsters from social service departments and probation offices, we were made even more aware of the 'wealth' that God had given us.

The first such group was a local one. They spent a week on board at the time when Graham and David were looking after the barge. Previously the barge had been used by church youth groups and their stay on board was often a second holiday. What would it be like to have youngsters on probation as our guests? They turned out to be better behaved than most church groups and thoroughly enjoyed the week. This was not just a second holiday for them — it was the first holiday that some of them had ever had.

Of course, not every group was as 'easy' as that first one, but they were always rewarding, despite the hard work. Some of our volunteer instructors found that taking a group sailing faced them with new challenges which had nothing to do with sailing prowess.

Tim found his crew neatly dressed in studded leather jackets and Doctor Marten boots (DMs). It was hardly the sort of gear for sailing, but there was no way they could be persuaded to change. It is hard enough to part someone from his DMs just to go to bed, let alone to go sailing!

Eventually they were persuaded to wear life-jackets and to get into the boat. But they refused to do anything towards helping sail the boat. They pretended boredom and indifference, when in fact they were probably quite scared, and they set off up the creek with Tim working the boat single-handed.

As they left the creek the wind picked up a bit, the crew's nonchalant air began to fade, and one of them began to look positively green. Beating out to sea, Tim gave the order to 'ready about', to which he received variations on 'Get lost, mate!'

Tim, who was getting rather exasperated by this time, replied, 'In that case you can all get out now and walk home.'

'Wot, 'ere?'

'We're in the middle of the sea!'

'Well, either you help,' said Tim, 'or you can go over the side. I'm not sailing the thing all by myself.'

As the sea got choppier, the boat began to take water in over the bows — it is surprising how much can come in if you try — and the crew began to look a little concerned.

'The wind is getting up,' said Tim sweetly. 'I think it's going to get much worse!'

'Aw, c'mon, we wanna go 'ome,' said one of them.

'Well, you'd better start helping then, hadn't you?'

At last they began to pay attention to Tim's instructions, as they struck a bargain that he would get them back safely, and preferably dry.

They had been scared stiff from the beginning. Now they were petrified — and learning a very important lesson. In some situations you have to do as you are told, no matter how averse to authority you may be; and there just may be some reason behind the orders given.

Sailing certainly is a great 'leveller'. They were all amazed next day that Tim was willing to take his crew out again, after the way they had treated him. But they were also pleased. They respected his sailing ability and knew they could trust him. This time they needed no persuasion to don life-jackets and get in the boat, and they were even keen to help rig it. After all, they knew a bit about this sailing lark now and did not need to cover up their fear. By the end of the day, two of the lads were helming quite well, and longing to come back.

Sailing in a Wayfarer with two or three other people broke down the larger gang. There was often a good opportunity for a chat and confidences, especially on a broad reach with not much happening. If Wayfarer masts could talk they would surely be able to share a great many secrets. And once an instructor has won the initial respect of a group, as Tim did, he grows in stature in his crew's eyes, and has a right to talk about what makes him tick as a person.

We were often surprised at the impact *Memory* seemed to have on some of these more difficult youngsters. The environment, as well as the sailing, was a great leveller. Things which we took for granted could be a bit of a culture shock to many youngsters. Fortunately that seemed to work in our favour, diluting the problems with a potentially difficult group.

There is usually one person who wants to be the leader and make trouble, in order to look big. On one occasion one particular girl was being extremely difficult and bolshy. At the start of the weekend everyone is always told the few 'standing orders' that we have. One of these is that all boats are out of bounds unless we are about to sail. We are constantly aware of the dangers of the sea and the need for safety and supervision.

Karen thought that this was a silly rule, and quickly jumped down onto the rescue boat. Then, before anyone could utter a word, she leapt out onto the mud, not realizing that she was not on solid ground, and thinking she could make good her escape that way. In seconds she was up to her waist in mud and very frightened. She took a lot of getting out, since she had driven herself in with such force! For the rest of the weekend Karen was rather quiet — and no trouble at all.

As time went by, certain individuals began to make a real impact on our lives, mainly because Fellowship Afloat had obviously made an impact on theirs. The one who probably influenced our thinking and actions most was Brian. Through him we came to see the tremendous need for long-term commitment to people whose lives had been damaged. We also discovered just how difficult that was, and how hard it was to reach and really help youngsters like this.

Brian came to Tollesbury for two weeks. He arrived on Friday evening, when a group from Harlow was due to come down for the weekend. After they had arrived, he quickly made up his mind that they were not his sort of people and decided to stay in his cabin. He threatened to run away but when we asked where he would go he did not know, because his parents were on holiday.

'Anyway,' he grunted, 'the police would soon catch up with me.'

After a lot of convincing, he ate his evening meal and then David and Tony took him up to the sailing club, where there was a party night. This seemed to be a bit more his scene and helped him to settle down.

The following day he went sailing with the group and began to get to know them, and seemed to be more at home with everyone. By the time the group left, he was really sad to see them go.

During the week Brian worked on *Ada*, the safety boat. He was always keen to start something but needed much encouragement to finish it. In the evening, David took him to visit various families, and it was obvious that Brian was quite overcome by the welcome and caring that he received.

One evening he said to David, 'Odd, yer kno', the people down 'ere speak nicer than even yer relatives.'

It was no surprise that by the end of the week he wanted to stay in Tollesbury for ever. He said he felt as if he'd been blind and now was able to see. It was like being alive after he had been dead. New horizons were being opened to him and, as the inevitable disagreements came, he began to realize that he never took other people's feelings or desires into consideration. Brian was doing a lot of new thinking.

At the weekend, Brian went cruising with the Fellowship. He sailed on most of the boats that went out, including the smack, and enjoyed the welcome he received on each one. He was very keen on sailing and wanted to become one of our volunteer sailing instructors. When the time finally came for him to return home, he was very reluctant to leave.

Three weeks later he came back. He was very anxious about his home situation and wanted to stay in Tollesbury. He even tried to persuade Keith and Gerry to adopt him. This was when we began to realize more of Brian's problems.

Life so far had really not treated him well. As a baby he had been put into care, when his father could not cope by himself. He was reasonably settled in his foster-home and was visited regularly by his father. One day his world was shattered by his father's announcement that he was going to marry Janie, the eldest daughter in the foster-home. So his father had not been coming to visit him. It was his foster-sister he had been interested in.

Brian went back to live with his father but it was not a recipe for success. It is hardly surprising that from the time he was eleven he was in and out of one institution after another, including Borstal.

Brian would say, 'People don't wanna kno' me, yer kno'. I'm just a Borstal boy.'

He found it difficult to believe that anyone wanted him. He certainly did not feel wanted at home. When we heard, a few weeks later, that he had taken an overdose and was very seriously ill in hospital, that he had had no visits from his family and was causing chaos in the hospital, we felt so frustrated that we could not offer him what he really needed: a stable family home where he was loved and cared for and wanted.

It seemed that Fellowship Afloat was the only place where

Brian had settled. So his social worker persuaded David to let Brian return to Tollesbury for a fortnight. There was nowhere else for him to go. Brian was really pleased to be back again. He settled in with the group (they were scouts from East Grinstead) very quickly. He was a great help with the sailing and spent two days helming the rescue boat, as well as helping with some work on Tony's boat, *Galliard*.

Very proud of his efforts, he wanted to show Peter, one of the older boys from the group, what he had been doing. They got on board when no one was around, found a bottle of brandy in a cupboard and helped themselves to a drink. Brian had rather a lot and was much the worse for wear. Peter persuaded him to return to *Memory* and suggested he take it easy in his cabin.

Unaware of what had been happening, David called everyone into the saloon and then sent them all up to the sail-loft to collect various bits and pieces. Brian went with the rest and noticed David's car standing there.

'Come on, Pete,' he said. 'Let's drive back to the barge.'

'No, better not,' said Peter. 'That's not a good idea!'

'C'mon, it'll be great. We'll just drive down to the hard, then.'

Despite Peter's objections Brian got into the car, started it up and off he went. Unfortunately he crashed into a concrete post. An upstanding member of the local community came over to sort things out — only to be threatened by Brian.

Peter eventually got Brian back to the barge and told David all that had happened. Brian himself was quite sorry by this time. He stayed in his bunk, while David went to apologize for what had happened and spoke to the policeman who had come to sort things out.

Sadly, this meant the end of Brian's stay. He had broken his contract of trust. He was found a place in a home run by Church House Trust, where he was delivered the next day. But David promised Brian that he could still go on the trip to Ostend on *William Emily* which had been planned. This he did, and very much enjoyed all the new experiences that it brought.

Even though it did not seem possible to cope with Brian in

Tollesbury permanently, we still felt very responsible for him. We were very aware that what we could offer was not enough. Tony offered him a job in London, but the journey into the unknown was simply too much, and Brian disappeared.

Although we had lost touch we thought about Brian and prayed for him often. And we worried away at the problem of providing long-term help for boys like him. We felt certain that he was back in Borstal somewhere or, if not, temporarily surviving on a life of crime.

Meanwhile we were making relationships with other youngsters.

Paul first came to us on a Community Service Order, and nearly set fire to the barge while he was burning off paint at the stern. Now he was in Hollesly Bay Borstal, despite holding down a job for a while. Drink was a constant problem and was usually responsible for the fights and trouble these youngsters got into.

There were encouraging cases too. Steve (and others like him) came to the barge and after several visits seemed so 'normal' that we wondered why he was being referred to us. A chat with his social worker revealed that before he came he appeared to be 'on the slippery slope downwards'. A year later, his school was much encouraged by his improved attendance, attitude and appearance; and things at home had settled down. Much of this was due to his visits to the barge.

So we came to see that there were young people whom we could help to see something better in life and inspire them to aim for it, even though there were some who were so damaged by the blows life had dealt them that odd visits were not enough. They needed a much deeper commitment.

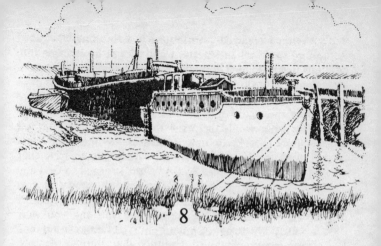

8

Brian

We heard nothing of Brian for over a year. Then we discovered that he was residing in Rochester Borstal.

During that time David and I had got married and set up home in our flat overlooking the waterside. We had also established an office in our spare bedroom. I was now teaching in the village.

On board *Memory* we had a new Bosun — Alan. He was to stay longer than the usual year. We had had a resident cook for the whole of one summer and were looking forward to appointing Kathy as the new resident in the spring. She would bring to us not only culinary delights but also musical ones. Paul was due to join us as Chief Sailing Instructor. So our full-time staff would be increased to four.

The memory of Brian was still strong and we could easily picture his face. When we heard the news, David sat down and wrote him a letter. So our friendship began again. It was as if there had been no gap. Tollesbury was obviously in his thoughts a great deal.

There came a time when we received this letter:

'The other day when I received your letter I was feeling down in the dumps and your letter really helped cheer me up.

'After I received your letter I was thinking what am I going to do when I get out and lots of ideas came into my head. Then I thought none of them are no good I would be inside again within a year. Then I thought of you and said to myself woulden it be grand if I could go down there and live and work at Tollesbury. Its the thing what would help me the most and sort me out because everybody down there is so open and kind hearted and helpful they dont care about my past they take me at face value. So that night I turned to God and prayed for him to help me show me the way and next morning I received a letter from my probation officer saying that he had been talking to you and you were seriously thinking of giving me accommodation and employment you dont know how that uplifted my faith in God. I'm not banking on it as you might not think I will not fit in there but do please think it over seriously I garrantee I will be of no hinderance whatsoever you wont regret it if you decide to take me on. But I'm still going to pray and hope.'

The letter sounded hopeful — except for the fact that it began by saying that Brian had got into trouble for bringing drugs into the Borstal, and was facing the possibility of a further eighteen months to three years inside.

Was he manipulating us? Probably. All the same, David went and spoke for him in court, and as a result Brian kept his target date for release. He would be coming to Tollesbury.

The problem of accommodation was acute. Eventually we decided he would have to live with us to begin with, sharing a room with the office. It was not the most ideal of situations, but the best we could do.

So, as our busy summer weeks came to an end, we prepared for Brian to join us. Alan's one-year term as Bosun was coming to an end, and he really had no plans for the future, so we decided to continue to employ him to undertake the enormous amount of maintenance work that was needed on *Memory*. When Brian arrived he would work with Alan and receive pocket-money. Again, it was far from ideal, but it was all we could offer. And Brian was so excited at the thought of being in Tollesbury again, he was full of promises that it would work. The promises were sincere enough — though we were full of fears that he would be unable to keep them.

Within one week it seemed as if everything was about to fall down around our ears. Living at such close quarters it was easy to 'keep an eye on' Brian. But it was understandable that he found the constraints difficult. He went out for one or two evenings and, although he returned at a reasonable time, we found ourselves behaving like anxious parents, listening for the click of the door as he came in.

On Friday night it was 2 a.m. before he came home. The next day there was quite a large amount of money and cigarettes stashed away in his cupboard, which he made no attempt to conceal. It was as if he wanted to be challenged.

When we heard that the newspaper shop in the village had been broken into, it was not hard to put two and two together.

We spent hours talking to Brian over numerous cups of coffee. He was very uptight and sullen, but eventually admitted that he was responsible.

'Well, you must go to the police,' said David.

'No fear, they'll have to come to me,' said Brian. 'You tell them.'

'No, Brian,' said David. 'I'm not going to tell them, you are. Don't you see that you stand a chance of being treated leniently if you confess?'

'No, I don't. I'll just be sent down again!'

'I don't think so. You must know the police by now. If you tell them all about it, you'll get off lightly.'

'I can't. Anyway, there was someone else and I'm not a grass.'

At first Brian refused to say anything about his 'partner in crime', but eventually David persuaded him that they should both go round to the lad's house and fetch him back to the flat to talk.

I phoned Keith and Gerry, and they said that they would come over straight away.

The whole story was really quite pathetic. It was obvious

that both boys had been drinking the previous night. It did not take too long to persuade them that the best plan was to call the police and tell their story. The village lad seemed quite happy as long as it was our local 'bobby' but he was frightened at the thought of the policeman from the next village. As it turned out, he was the one on duty, and when he came over with a colleague, they clearly did not know what to make of us. The solution to a crime was not often handed to them on a plate, and they could not quite believe what was happening.

The police agreed to call us when they had finished their questioning. It was more than likely that the lads would be allowed home, and we would pick them up and bring them back. It was two very quiet lads we collected from the police-station at 2.30 a.m.

Brian was given an eighteen-month sentence, suspended for six months. That meant he had to stay out of trouble for six months, or was likely to be sent down. With this hanging over his head, and the feeling that he had let us down so soon, it is not surprising that there were tensions from time to time. But considering Brian's background, our small home, and our busy, erratic lives, he coped with surprising ease.

The battles were almost always over the time he returned home and the problem of too much alcohol. We never reached an amicable conclusion: normally Brian simply stormed off. It was fortunate that he had a number of boltholes. He could visit Kathy or Paul in the village, or go down to the barge to visit the new Bosun (Mike) and Alan. It was a pity that these escapes were all to people involved in working for Fellowship Afloat, because there were many more tensions within Brian's work situation. The authority structure in Fellowship Afloat was very flexible — it had not needed to be otherwise — and Brian found that very difficult to cope with. His attitude towards work and people was very impatient and he found it almost impossible to accept guidance or direction from anyone other than David.

The main work continued while Brian was with us, and a great many things happened. We had our first-ever barn dance in the village, our first fishing weekend, and our first medieval banquet, complete with medieval music.

Just before Brian had come to live with us, we had been to see *Plain Kate*, a fine, old wooden 'between-the-wars' motor cruiser, now without her engine and moored in the creek at the little village of St Osyth. We had heard about her more than a year before, but the asking price, though cheap, was much more than we could afford, and we had forgotten about her. In any case, we were at that stage planning to augment our accommodation with a steel barge which we had found lying in Plymouth and had bought for £1,100. After an eighteen-month wait for a tow that we could afford, we were again offered *Plain Kate*. So we decided to try to sell the barge at Plymouth. This brought in £1,600, which enabled us to consider *Plain Kate*.

When we saw her, we fell in love with her. It was quite obvious that she was exactly what we needed for extra accommodation for the increasing number of volunteers who were coming down each weekend to help. We had been sleeping people in the sail-loft. And her lovely old upholstered saloon would provide a cosy — and necessary — escape from it all.

Once more, as we looked back, we could see God's hand in it all. The extra money raised by buying and then selling the Plymouth barge had made the ideal purchase possible. How very practically God provides, and how perfectly he times things.

We set aside a day in November for bringing *Plain Kate* round to Tollesbury. We were going to use our faithful old *Ada* to tow her and we needed good weather with not much wind.

The day dawned bright and clear, and Brian was as excited as any of us as the party set off. Brian revelled in this kind of activity. He took as much pride in *Plain Kate* as we did, and was just as anxious for her safety, keeping an eye on her moorings in her new mud-berth just ahead of *Memory*.

But no job is full of 'highs' and Brian's main problem was coping with more mundane tasks and seeing them through. He felt he had to insist that he knew best, and it was often much like dealing with a very young child. This was difficult to cope with. It was inevitable that eventually he should seek alternative employment.

He found it with a local electronics firm. The job was not altogether suitable, since it was very routine. But he settled in quite well, coming home with exaggerated tales of his speed in doing things, and how he amazed everyone.

Once Brian was no longer working for the Fellowship, some of the tensions at home eased, although we still worried if he was late. He had begun to make many acquaintances in the village, largely through the public houses, but these relationships were tinged with fear. People were always unsure how he would react to situations. He presented himself as a 'big toughie' with others in a way that he did not do with us.

During this time we felt we were living with two different people.

When there was a crisis, or he had had too much to drink, Brian became sullen and uncommunicative. He would be angry and explosive and completely unreasonable.

At other times he was a very attractive and lively person. He could recognize his 'other self' and talk about it, revealing a very deep insight and understanding of his personality and predicament. He had a great sense of humour, and was very intelligent and gifted artistically. He felt he had potential really to make something of his life. But somehow he did not know how to achieve what he wanted.

There were so many 'ifs' in Brian's life but certainly, if there had been no drink, it would have made a lot of difference. He would promise faithfully not to drink too much — he knew the effect it would have on him, he would be full of good intentions, and he was in fact quite capable of going out for an evening and coming back sober.

We should have realized trouble was brewing when he came home from work and said that he had been given a week's notice over a dispute about bonuses. He was always saying how much faster he worked than anyone else, but either the management did not believe him, or they had twigged that he was exaggerating his output. He was angry

74

about it, but quite sure he could get another job soon enough.

Usually we could tell if he was bent on trouble, but this time he seemed very much his normal self.

It was a Friday night and Brian went out as usual. We heard him come down the hill on his small Honda at about 2 a.m. I suppose we were just relieved that he was safely home, and had not got involved in a fight or fallen off his bike. The next day Brian stayed in bed late and seemed his usual self when he got up. We had no idea that his activities of the previous evening had been disastrous.

That afternoon the local policeman presented himself at the door and asked if Brian was in. The previous night, probably in the small hours of the morning, the local firm where Brian had been working had been broken into and about £2,000-worth of damage done. The circumstantial evidence pointed to Brian, and examination of his clothing would soon prove it. He had also left a lovely footprint with his brand-new DMs. We asked the policeman in and Brian seemed to be expecting him. He went off to the police-station without a word.

Our feelings were indescribable. It was obviously the end of every chance Brian had with us in Tollesbury. We had been living on a knife-edge for so long that we could not help feeling a certain sense of relief. We had often wondered how much longer we could go on coping. Now the decision had been taken out of our hands. But we were desperately sad and disappointed. Over and over we asked ourselves if there was something more we could have done that would have made things different.

We were grateful that people in the village were so sympathetic and understanding. They might easily have resented the fact that we had brought Brian to Tollesbury.

Our friendship with Brian continued by letter — to a variety of prisons. David visited him in Wormwood Scrubs. Brian regretted what had happened and was very hopeful for the future. Later, from Camp Hill on the Isle of Wight, he wrote:

'Well, I've been thinking and taking a good look at myself, and I do not like what I see, let's be frank — while I was staying with you in Tollesbury I was a right out and out b____. Sorry, but it's true, and I cannot find no other word to describe myself and my actions.

'...wouldn't it have been great to have someone who would have helped around the flat...someone you could have felt success with. But that wasn't me. I thought I was tough, hard, cool but what a fool, I had something really good going for me and I chose to blow it sky high.'

A year after he left us, Brian was released on a Friday. He was back inside on Saturday. We could hardly believe it. This time it seemed he would be charged with assaulting a policeman. The charge was reduced but he still faced another eighteen months in prison, in Stafford and Nottingham.

Then one night we had a phone-call from him. He was in a hostel in Leamington Spa and had been there for six weeks. We were going across to Gloucestershire within the next two weeks, so we promised to visit him, and also take him his little motor-bike. Hopefully, getting it on the road again would give him something to do. The prospects for a job did not sound good.

We had a good visit, and a long talk with the warden in charge of the hostel. Brian had quite a lot going for him in Leamington. But even if he had found a job it is doubtful whether he would have lasted long without getting into trouble. He really needed a job that was challenging and exciting, doing something different every day, so that he did not need to turn to crime to get his 'kicks'.

It was frustrating and heartbreaking but no real surprise when we received the next letter in the familiar handwriting on Her Majesty's stationery, this time from Birmingham. Brian pointed out that he had lasted four months!

The saddest letter we had from Brian came some months and several fresh escapades later:

'...just to say thankyou for the help and assistance in the past that you have giving me. I think all in all you have helped me more than anyone in my life, and although I may not show it I do appreciate it. I do wish to God sometimes that there wasnt in me a self-destructive element that wishes to destroy everything people do for me!...

'I think you at fellowship afloat once showed me the right road but I was to blind and stupid to see it. I wish I knew and felt then what I do now. Nobody's going to help me now, we dissipointed to many people thrown away to many chances.'

If that had been the last we heard of Brian we would have been sad indeed, but the next time he was released from prison, he actually stayed out of trouble. We had several happy telephone-calls from him, first while he was staying in London and later when he went down to Cornwall. He said that he was earning a good living as a portrait artist and that he had settled down with a lovely Cornish family that he had got to know.

After that we heard from him from time to time, and every so often he expressed a desire to come to Tollesbury and talked of buying a house-boat. We thought he was settled and happy.

He had been out of trouble for over a year when we received a telephone-call telling us that Brian had shot himself. The question we all asked but could not answer was, 'Why?'

Knowing Brian influenced our thinking a great deal. It made us see the impossibility of being able to help some youngsters without some kind of residential community, which we do not have at the barge. It taught us a lot, making us more prepared for the inevitable disappointments and let-downs. We were glad we had known Brian. For all our lack of skill and inadequacy, we knew that we had been able to give him something which he had found nowhere else, and which he never forgot. The rest we can only leave to God.

9

Tidal Disaster

'There's hardly any water in the creek!' said David, as he came in, bringing a blanket of cold with him, and pulled off his waterproofs.

It was after the Fellowship had bought *Plain Kate* and while Brian was still with us. Mike had succeeded Alan as Bosun.

'But it ought to be well up by now, surely!' I exclaimed.

David had been out to check *Memory*'s moorings. The winds were so strong we feared that when the tide came up she might break loose.

'Yes, I know. There's going to be hardly any tide at all; I've never seen the creek so empty, half an hour before the top of the tide.'

'Why is that, do you think?' I asked.

'I suppose this south-easterly is holding the water back in the North Sea. Let's just hope it doesn't shift round. Tonight's tide is supposed to be higher than this one.'

'Oh dear. That doesn't sound so good. Still, I'd better get back to school. See you later.'

When Brian came in that evening, he was so excited I thought that the high winds were affecting him, the way they affected the children at school. They had been almost uncontrollable that afternoon.

'It's going to be a really big tide, isn't it?' said Brian. 'Will it come over the bridge?'

'I don't know,' replied David, 'but I don't think we'll be going to bed. The wind has shifted round, and it's getting stronger every minute. I think I'll ring the coastguard.'

A few minutes later he returned and said, 'There's a flood alert. I think I'll go and have a look around. Won't be long.'

'I'll come too,' said Brian, and they both went out. I was glad it was not me. The noise of the wind was so menacing, the whole flat seemed to shake. I was quite glad when they both returned.

'We couldn't get down to the barge,' said Brian.

'You must be able to,' I said. 'The tide isn't due for another three hours.'

'We couldn't get down,' said David. 'The tide is well over the path — too deep for waders. It's going to be the most massive tide.'

'Do you think Mike is all right?' I asked.

'I should think so. I'm just going to give him a ring. Don't worry,' he added, seeing my worried face. 'He'll be all right.'

Mike reported that waves were crashing against *Memory*, some of the hatches had blown off and disappeared, and the Wayfarer had hopped on top of the pontoons. Why, oh why, had we kept a dinghy in the water this winter? It would be wrecked. Mike had managed to get the boat back in the water, but the operation had been a bit frightening, and it would probably happen again.

'I think I'll keep my life-jacket on,' said Mike down the telephone. 'It's pretty hairy here.'

Poor Mike. I was concerned about him, all by himself down there.

'What will he do if the barge breaks loose?' I said.

'Don't worry,' said David, always optimistic. 'He'll be all right. We checked the moorings and put that new one down the other day. Mike'll be all right.'

'I wish I was down there,' said Brian. 'I bet it's really good with the Tillys swinging and the wind howling.'

Being dark made everything more frightening, and as the waves came up the road, beating against the piers of the sail-lofts, it seemed as though nothing could stop the onslaught of the sea. Very soon the water was lapping the flood-boards that had been put across the road, where the sea-wall is breached at the humpy-backed bridge. David and Brian were just about to go out again when there was a knock at the door.

'Can you come? *Tranton*'s broken loose.'

Tranton was an eighty-foot ex-Air Sea Rescue boat, now used as a house-boat, and the young couple who lived on board really believed their home was lost. She had come right up onto the hard standing, and was in danger of tipping over into the creek as the tide ebbed.

David and Brian and four others spent an hour with their backs pressed firmly to the side, keeping her away from the bank. She would still be perched at a peculiar angle, but everyone was exhausted. *Tranton* would have to be left until the next tide, daylight and an available motor-boat.

Meanwhile I was sitting by the telephone, keeping in touch with Mike. He was beginning to fear the worst.

Memory rose higher and higher. It would not be long before she rose above the security of the pier and broke loose.

High tide should have been at one o'clock, but it was then 2.30 and showed no signs of turning.

There was nothing Mike could do when the pontoon and the Wayfarer lodged themselves on top of the old piles of the pier. It would have been much too dangerous to try.

That was the first and only time Mike slept in his life-jacket, or rather, prayed and dozed as he sat in the warmth and shelter of the master's cabin.

Eventually he telephoned to say, 'I think the tide has turned. There's nothing else I can do till morning. I think I'll turn in. This must be the most exciting night I've ever spent on *Memory*.'

Not long afterwards the telephone rang again.

'The tide's coming back in!' Mike's voice on the other end sounded awe-struck. 'I can't believe it! And the wind! I just crawled about on deck on all fours, or I'd have been over the side. It'll be a miracle if we don't break loose now!'

Gale force winds had piled up the water, and whereas the earlier tide had been kept back, this tide seemed to have another surge, as if the water had all been heaped up.

I felt as if it would never go away. But at last David and Brian came in and reported that it had turned and was going out quite quickly.

'I'm a bit worried about Ann on the ferro-boat,' said David. 'Can we have a quick cup of tea? As soon as we can get down the path we'll go and see if she is all right.'

Ann and her husband, Bob, had been fitting-out a ferro-cement boat and living on it at the same time. The boat was moored in a mud-berth on the edge of Gridiron Creek quite near to *Memory*, and was really quite exposed. Bob was out in Gibraltar and Ann was alone on the boat.

It was an enormous struggle for David and Brian to get to the boat. They had to negotiate other boats, straddled across the path. And on leaving the path to cross the bridge over a small creek, the only way to get to Ann's boat, they found the bridge gone. At least, it had collapsed, and it was only by executing a slippery balancing act that it was possible to get across. Then, when they neared the ferro-boat, their hearts sank. It had come half out of its berth and was perched at a very dangerous angle. It was a miracle it had not fallen over.

One shout brought a reply from Ann, who was so relieved to see someone.

It's hard to imagine what it must have been like to be down below. The boat, although supposedly moored safely in a mud-berth, rocked at alarming angles, with the wind screaming above. Then, after an eternity, a sudden stillness as the boat was caught up on the bank with the tide going out. A final violent crash and the boat heeled over, throwing everything to the other side of the cabin.

No wonder Ann was pleased to see David and Brian. She was even more pleased to accept an invitation to come ashore and return to the flat with them, even though she could not see how she was going to get off the boat. It was tipped over into the creek, so the gunwales were a long way from the bank. However, they managed between them, and David felt fairly certain that the boat was safe for the time being. So they were soon negotiating the broken bridge.

There were not many hours of the night left when we eventually went to bed. Minutes later, it seemed, I had to get up and go to school.

With the daylight, we could see the full extent of the damage. It was unbelievable. It looked as if a giant had

81

picked up all the boats and tossed them around. They were strewn at random over the saltings.

There were boats tipped at all sorts of odd angles. Some seemed to have disappeared altogether but were rediscovered in the most amazing positions.

Many were high and dry, on top of the marshes. It would need a really good tide to float them off. A steel barge was straddled across one of the creeks. All the boats that had been moored on the western side of the path now either straddled the path, were on the far side, or nowhere to be seen. A *Debutante* that belonged to a friend had blown right across the saltings to the road, and smashed one of its bilge keels on the concrete entrance to the boatyard.

Only *Memory* and *Plain Kate* were sitting in their berths as if the previous night had not happened. The only evidence that the winds had come anywhere near was the pontoons and orange *Wayfarer*, perched up on the pier. We were so thankful to God for keeping *Memory* safe. If she had broken loose and been swept across the creek to be washed up on the opposite bank at some awkward angle, it is doubtful that she could have survived.

During the day there was another enormous tide, but the winds had died down considerably, and it was possible to do some rescuing of boats. It was a pity not all the boat-owners could come and rescue their craft straight away. The tide would not be high enough again to enable them to do so easily.

David, Brian, Alan and Mike concentrated their efforts where the need was greatest.

Ann's boat was in great danger of tipping over, since her decks would be awash before she floated. It was touch and go whether or not they would be able to pull her upright before the water found its way below.

It was a great relief when she was floating again and could be properly moored in her berth.

There was one nasty moment when Ann discovered water in the engine-room.

'Have you tasted it?' asked David. 'Is it fresh?' Thankfully it was, and fears of a leak were allayed.

Tranton was persuaded back into her berth and made

secure. The young couple on board had to rethink the way she was moored. The strain on her lines as the tide rose higher and higher, combined with the force of the wind against her, must have been enormous.

Our pontoons and dinghy were rescued. The pontoons needed repair; the dinghy a new mast. Later in the day, Mike and Brian went for a walk around the sea-wall, where a great deal of 'flotsam and jetsam' had appeared. There they were delighted to find a missing hatch from the barge. So our losses were minimal, and we were deeply grateful for God's care.

10

Sanderling

Our faithful motor boat *Ada*, which acted as rescue-boat every time the fleet of Wayfarers went out, was soon going to be in need of rescuing herself. She was an ex-Naval cutter, clinker-built, with a two-cylinder diesel engine. She afforded very little shelter from the elements, having only a small cuddy at the front. Her engine made so much noise we had to shout to be heard above it. But she was invaluable to us.

Every so often *Ada* would have to have some repair work done. We even considered sheathing her in concrete to ensure that her hull would be watertight. One day, when David had taken a group sailing across to Mersea and they were having their coffee break, some people David vaguely knew asked if he would take them out to their moored boat. When they were half-way between shore and boat David looked down to see *Ada*'s floorboards totally awash. And the depth of water was increasing visibly.

'I think we had better go back,' David said. And no one countered the suggestion!

Thankfully they reached the shore. David beached the boat and looked to see where the water was coming in. There was a hole in the hull which must have been caused by something sharp which had caught the boat the first time he had come ashore. It was obvious that the group was not going to get back to Tollesbury with a leak like that. So David went off to find materials for a repair.

He returned with some lead and copper nails to make a 'tingle'. Then the group put their backs to the boat, to hold it up while he fixed the patch. They returned to Tollesbury without further incident. But it was yet another reminder that *Ada*'s hull was anything but sound. We ought to be looking for a replacement before disaster struck. With six Wayfarer dinghies to look after, she had quite a responsibility on the water, and by now we were running field study courses and fishing trips through the winter, so she was always needed for something. Although she had never yet failed to be there when needed, she really was not trustworthy any more.

The pressing need for a new rescue-vessel was a big problem. Our slender budget did not allow for such a large capital outlay, and we puzzled over many vague possibilities.

About this time, our concern for the needs of Brian and others like him, led us to enquire about job-creation schemes, as a possible way of funding the extra employment we wanted to offer. We knew that the Mayflower Family Centre in London's East End was setting up such a scheme. So David decided that it would be a good idea to talk to them about what they were doing.

We could hardly believe our ears when we discovered that they were setting up a project to build ferro-cement hulls. The initial plan was to build a large, forty-five-foot motor-cruiser, which they would then fit-out and use, and a smaller twenty-five-foot fishing-boat. This latter boat was a bit of a problem, because they did not know what to do with it. At that time they were not allowed to sell it. Yet they could not give it away to just anybody. And who would want a twenty-five-foot ferro-cement hull, with all the work of fitting-out still to be done?

We quickly told them. It was exactly what Fellowship Afloat wanted. They were delighted. We would be an ideal recipient for the hull, and as the design had not yet been settled, we could actually have the boat designed to fit our needs in Tollesbury.

We forgot all about job creation projects for ourselves, as we got involved in the planning for the one in Canning Town.

This was the beginning of a very close relationship between the Mayflower Centre and ourselves, with David driving there at least once a month. It was interesting to see the progress as the frames were made out of steel and then fastened together with stringers to form the shape of the boat. This was all then covered with several layers of mesh to form the skeleton of the boat, ready to be plastered.

Then came the plastering party, with everyone giving a hand. Provided there was plenty to eat and numerous cups of tea and coffee, everyone was ready to help mix and move all the concrete that was necessary to finish the hull. A team of professional plasterers came in to do the final really skilled bit, which was smoothing off the outside.

When the day for the plastering of our boat arrived, Bob, Brian, Alan, David and I set off at the crack of dawn. I made sure that I was more involved with the tea and coffee than with the concrete, as I entered a world of frenzied activity.

The mix had to be just right. The dry ingredients and the water went into the mixer. Then the buckets of cement were hauled up into the boat and passed to a team. They filled the keel first. This had to be done extremely carefully.

After that, the concrete had to be pressed onto the inside of the boat and pushed through the mesh. This was when the plasterers came into their own. They would put a nice smooth finish on the outside. The most important thing was to keep the concrete coming.

There was only one rule about eating and drinking — no tea or coffee in the boat. Apparently someone once had a hole fall out of their concrete hull because a cup of coffee had been spilt in it. Sugar does something to the setting properties!

How different the boat looked, all plastered up, and how much bigger. She seemed so broad in the beam, and her stern looked strange, sloping inwards towards the top. Now we would have to wait for her to 'cure'. It was important for the concrete not to dry out too quickly, so the boat would have to be kept wet for some time. We could hardly wait for her to come to Tollesbury!

She arrived in March 1978. The hull sat there on the hard-standing, dark and grey, and for a while aroused much comment and suspicion — it was doubted by many that she would actually float.

Once the excitement had died down, reality took over. There stood what could only be described as a 'grey elephant'. A hull is not much good unless it has, at least, an engine, and it was apparent that a lot of money and effort were still needed.

However, with typical optimism, everyone was sure that the boat would soon be in commission, and that the old rescue-launch's days were numbered. Convinced that only the best was good enough, enquiries were made about purchasing a new three-cylinder Lister diesel engine, and already there were dreams of chugging out into the estuary with everything imaginable on board — cooker for brewing up, Elsan loo, the comfort and protection of a wheel-house; there was even some talk of radar. No more would the helmsman stand in the stern of the boat, battered by the elements, wishing that he could at least make himself a cup of tea. But these were only dreams. Or were they?

The autumn came round and we still had not made a start. David had been doing a great deal of planning but, without any funds, there seemed little we could do.

By now we were very involved with disadvantaged youngsters who came to us via the social services and probation office. Our centre was ideal for them. Here they found challenge, a chance to succeed at something new, an opportunity to be with people who cared and who had a very different code for living from what they were used to. On the strength of this we applied to a government fund for a grant towards fitting-out the boat. The application was successful, and by October we had the £6,500 we needed to fit-out the boat.

This put a completely new complexion on things. Now we could purchase the engine and get to work. Very quickly a boat-shed was designed and erected. 'Boat-shed' is a rather glorious title for the polythene greenhouse that we put up. It was an enormous structure. It had to be high enough to accommodate the wheel-house and provide room for storage and working area. It was made in sections that were then put up around the boat.

The day we chose to put it together, there was such a gale blowing that I expected the whole lot to take off, ourselves with it. Even I was called in to join the battle with Steve, Bosun Jeremy, and David. All hands were needed to hold the huge sections in place, tie them down and fasten them together.

Once more we seemed to be making progress. The shed withstood the first of the winter gales, and we began to gather materials. Soon we were preparing the laminates for the deck-beams and then waiting for the temperature in the sail-loft to reach 50°F so that we could actually start laminating. Somehow Jeremy, our current bosun, managed to get all the deck-beams made, in between all his other jobs, and with help from some of the volunteers and youngsters who came down.

The next task was to fit a tank underneath the deck to take the effluent from our long-promised and not-yet-installed 'super-loos' — a job which Stuart undertook and completed. This would then mean that waste was easily pumped out into the estuary. But somehow, with all the busyness of activities on board the barge, looking after the groups who came down each weekend, and the maintenance that was needed to run the centre, plus a project to fit-out the forecabin of *Plain Kate* with six bunks, nothing else very noticeable happened to the lonely concrete hull. We began to feel that we should never find time to get the boat finished, and there were jokes about growing tomatoes in that 'shed' instead.

It soon became obvious that someone would have to be employed to undertake the bulk of the work. Finances were already stretched but money was promised, and Alan agreed to come back to take on the task.

A year and a half after its arrival in Tollesbury the hull began to look less like an empty shell. Gradually the deck-beams went in and disappeared under the deck, a wheel-house grew, the engine went in, and all the little things that no one noticed were being completed: tanks and skin-fittings, batteries, bilge-runners... It was very exciting to see the object of much planning actually taking shape, and we began to believe that she would be in the water in the spring.

For Alan, doing most of the work, and for David, the biggest problem was design. We did not want to end up with a monstrosity. Because the boat was inside the shed it was not possible to stand back and look at her lines. In desperation, they made a huge cardboard cut-out of the wheel-house as they thought it should be, put it on the boat, and then waited for darkness to fall, so that they could put a powerful light behind it and stand back to observe the effect!

When we reached the stage of painting the hull, I used to go and help. It was such a huge expanse and all the epoxy paint had to be mixed at once, so it needed all hands to apply it before the paint went off.

At last we had a launch-date in view: Easter Monday, 1980. To make sure we met our deadline, we decided to ask a well-known show-biz personality to do the honours. To our great delight, Roy Castle agreed to come and make our day a very special one.

Work reached a feverish pitch. She really began to look like a boat, with her smart wheel-house with its orange coach-roof and windows, and big rubber fendering. The engine and stern gear were installed but there was still the steering and control system to fit.

It was imperative that we settled on a name; we could not very well launch her without one. We felt it would be nice to name her after one of the birds we were so familiar with on the saltings. We settled for *Sanderling*.

We hoped that the day of the launch would be a special one for Tollesbury, as well as for us. It is not very often now that a boat is built and launched in Tollesbury, and although *Sanderling* was not exactly a traditional boat, she was a work-boat designed especially for our use, in and around the Blackwater. We booked the nearby scout hut for a reception afterwards, and wondered whether we would be able to fit everyone in.

The ends of the boat-shed were taken down in preparation for the boat to be moved. At last we could stand back and admire her. The next problem was squeezing her out between the sail-lofts. It looked a tight fit, but she had gone in, so she must come out — her fenders could not have made her that much wider. After two years in that greenhouse, though, we would not have been surprised if she had taken root and grown!

We wanted to use the slip for the launching. It would provide a good setting for everyone to see what was happening, and it would seem more like a proper launching than pushing her off a trailer on the hard. The problem was that, to get onto the slip, she had to be in the water already.

So, a few days before the big day, we towed her down to the hard on the trailer and sent her off into the water. Everyone accused us of wanting to make sure she actually floated — people are very suspicious of concrete boats, and find it difficult to believe that they really do float. It was thrilling to see her in the water at last and somewhat of a relief to find that she would float more or less on her lines, once she was ballasted. We warped her round to the slip and the next day we were able to float her onto the carriage and haul her out. There was just time to paint on her water-line and anti-foul her.

Easter Monday dawned with a flurry of activity. The village was alive with excitement at the thought of our important visitor. We put up bunting everywhere, made last-minute checks on the rope that would pull *Sanderling* down the slip, and checked the tide-table a thousand times to make sure we had got the time right.

Would the tide come in far enough to float her when she was at the bottom of the slip? The day before, it had been smaller than the prediction. What an embarrassment if, on the big occasion, she did not actually get into the water!

The launch was due to take place at half past four. Hours beforehand people started to stream down the road and mill around, either side of the slope and up and down the road. We could hardly believe it. We had asked someone to provide a public address system for us, and he was pumping out music, so that it seemed like carnival time. *Sanderling*, the centre of attraction, sat proudly on the slip (with Alan on board, still frantically working).

Roy Castle arrived a good hour before the time of the launch, and went 'walkabout', speaking to as many people as possible and signing dozens of autographs. Everyone loved him.

The local press arrived and, as half past four drew nearer, people began moving into a good position to see everything.

We had a team of hefty volunteers, ready to haul on the rope. The speeches were made. Roy gave a moving prayer, dedicating the boat and all those who would use her to the service of God. Then, with a quick burst on his trumpet, he grabbed the bottle of champagne.

'I name this boat *Sanderling*!'

He swung the bottle at the bows, the signal for the boat to start its journey down the slip — and it missed!

'Oh dear!' he said. 'I've never done this before. Does the queen have this trouble?'

The second time there was a lovely splash of bubbly and we held our breath as the rope-crew started to heave. Slowly but surely *Sanderling* began to inch her way down the slip, to the cheers of the crowd and the grand tones of Roy's trumpet.

Then, horror of horrors, she came to a halt and, despite renewed efforts on the rope, she refused to budge.

The crowd fell silent. Roy changed his tune to 'The Last Post' and, as the crowd began to chuckle, he leapt to the ground, handed his trumpet and his jacket to an amazed bystander and, rolling up his sleeves, led David, Keith and Stuart down the slip and started pushing.

With a lurch *Sanderling* started to move again, and everyone waited with bated breath as she edged towards the water. A great cheer went up when she finally hit the water. And when she was well and truly floating we had another fanfare from Roy's trumpet.

Memory was not forgotten. Roy and many other visitors went down to see her. We served hundreds of cups of tea, and Roy must have signed as many autographs. We were grateful to him for making the day so memorable, and for giving God the thanks due to him for all his marvellous provision.

After a few sea trials and modifications, *Sanderling* was in commission. The first party to go out on her were the lads from the Mayflower Project who had built her hull.

11

Shocks and Surprises

1978, the year of the high tide and of *Sanderling*'s arrival as a bare grey hull, was certainly a year to remember.

The summer began with drama. A group from a probation office was on board. After the evening meal on Wednesday, we saw twenty or so Tollesbury youths stride down the path and line up in neat but threatening order along the lower gang-plank.

'We want Paul!' shouted the spokesman of the group.

The decks of *Memory* emptied in an instant and all that was to be seen were a few heads peering out of the hatches. There was much conversation and preparation down below for the Big Fight!

It took a few minutes for David and the others to gather their senses. Paul was a very vocal member of the group, with as much mouth as muscle. What had he been up to? He must have provoked this little visitation.

Making a few quick enquiries, David discovered that the group had gone to the village the previous evening and visited the local youth club. Paul had announced in no uncertain terms that he and his group were going to take the club over.

Quite apart from the fact that our group was outnumbered three to one, there was no way we were going to have a fight on our hands. The only alternative was an apology from Paul, but could he be persuaded to do that? The other youngsters quickly saw the wisdom of this line of action and brought sufficient pressure to bear on Paul to get him up on deck to face the enemy.

As Paul was escorted at arm's length down the gang-plank, the rest of the group crept out from their hatches to hear his quivering apology.

To our surprise, the members of the youth club said, 'Thanks — we accept,' and went home.

It was quite a relief to us — and certainly a lesson for Paul. He had been a real pain since he arrived, bullying everyone to give him cigarettes and preventing the whole group from settling down. Our efforts to deal with the problem had been nowhere near so successful as this little incident. Afterwards, since Paul's status with the group was somewhat shattered, we had a really successful week. It was good to be able to settle down and relax, and to be able to give some attention to others in the group.

If we had been able to see into the future we would have taken our holiday in the next two weeks, when things went really well on the barge, a great deal of fun was had by everyone, and there were no problems.

The next group to arrive came from Bath. We were a little apprehensive, as we did not know anything about them. We had never met the woman who was bringing them. We gathered from her correspondence that they were all youngsters off the street, to whom she had opened her home. We now know Hilary very well and look forward to her visits, but that first occasion was traumatic.

From the very beginning it was obvious we were going to have trouble. But how best to deal with it? It was the first time we had really encountered the problem of the resident group wanting to spend the evening in the pub, and we learnt a lot that week.

Most of the group were under age, but all of them were in the habit of going out for a drink. And for some of them Friday night, with a full pay-packet, was the time really to enjoy themselves — which meant getting drunk. Coming away on holiday, they considered that every night was Friday night.

After hauling them out of the pub on the first night, we talked to them for a long time. But we were obviously worlds apart. Why shouldn't they enjoy themselves? They were on

holiday, weren't they? We just wanted to spoil their fun.

Eventually they agreed to join in our planned activities and we agreed that those who were old enough to visit the pub could do so. But they were not to drink too much, and there was to be no drink on board.

We were not really surprised, though, when Jethro returned to the barge the next night very drunk, and we had to make the painful decision to send him home. It may seem a straightforward decision, when someone steps out of line, to discipline him. But when youngsters come from such an alien, insecure background, it is really quite difficult to be wise and do the right thing.

Undoubtedly, though, the right thing this time was to send Jethro home. It meant putting him on a train at Witham and giving him instructions on how to get across London on the underground and find the right train to get him to Bath. Jethro was well over eighteen, but he was really scared at the thought of getting through London by himself. A very quiet Jethro set out on his journey home, and a very subdued group was left behind.

The problem of someone arriving back on the barge drunk was an internal one for us to resolve. The following week we were very grateful to have the support of the village in our troubles.

We had planned a course for individuals from the local authorities and probation offices. Our activities included art and craft work, as well as sailing, and we had had a very enthusiastic response from social workers and probation officers, so much so that one probation officer joined us for the week, together with three clients from her office.

We had several very enthusiastic artists on board, with all sorts of ideas. Richard, a graphic designer, had planned the week, and persuaded some of his friends to join us. There was Taffy, who was really keen on cartoons, and John and Roger, whose skill with a pencil, and advice on sketching, inspired some of the youngsters to produce some amazing things.

We did lino-cutting and tie-dying, sketching and candle-making, stone-painting and screen-printing, with all sorts of fantastic designs and results. We were a little unorthodox — the emphasis was always on creativity. Using emulsion paint for screen-printing gave strange results. Having worked out a design, everyone wanted to see it printed onto a tee-shirt, front and back, and the finished article ended up rather stiff.

We also had some unusual candles. A hand with wicks coming out of the bright red finger-nails was rather horrible. After a lad called Roger had told us twenty times that he had got candle-wax on his Elvis Presley tee-shirt, and we had told him twenty times how to get it off, it seemed simpler to do it for him. He was like the needle of a record-player, stuck in a groove.

It was Roger who managed to get the red dye all over most of himself as well as the material when he was tie-dying. Then, of course, twenty times and more we heard about the red that would not come off his hands.

At the beginning of the week it did not look like being a great success. Although we had only nine youngsters on board, with a staff ratio of at least two to one, it was very hard work to get everyone to settle down. Two of the girls, who had eventually to be sent home, set out to be extremely difficult, refusing to eat or to take part in the activities, complaining about everything from the food to their beds, and generally trying to stir up everyone else.

It is difficult to know if the week could have been the success it became if those two girls had stayed. Their departure certainly changed the atmosphere completely.

My summer holiday from teaching was swiftly coming to an end, and David felt that the last week of the summer bookings was bound to go smoothly.

We had asked Graham Leavers to be our 'padre' for the week. He had got over that first visit to the barge, when he felt entirely overrun by dogs and babies. Even though he was extremely busy, he had often found time to talk to us about all that was happening on *Memory* and was always anxious to be involved. This time he not only agreed to come, he was very much looking forward to spending the time with us, and especially to going out sailing.

David and I had not booked a holiday. We intended to take our tent and head for Scotland. As each week of the summer had brought new drama, David had found it difficult to think in terms of leaving. It seemed as if every other day held a crisis. Surely this week would be straightforward? There was a group of individuals from various churches on board, all enthusiastic to sail and to absorb everything that was going on. By the middle of the week we felt we could safely disappear unnoticed.

But on Tuesday morning we were woken at half past

seven by the shrilling of the telephone.

'Something dreadful has happened.' The voice at the other end was barely audible. Then the receiver changed hands and we heard John's voice. He too was plainly in a state of shock. But what he said was clear enough.

Graham Leavers had died in his sleep.

We could hardly begin to take it in. It seemed silly to ask 'Are you sure?' But it was so totally unbelievable.

Time passed in a blur of telephone-calls and activity, as we called the doctor and then tried to contact someone whom we could ask to break the news to Graham's wife, Twink.

Graham had been planning to get up at seven o'clock and travel home, before visiting his doctor, with whom he had an appointment. He was sleeping in the saloon of *Plain Kate* and when John and Cathy, who were in the next cabin, realized that he was not up, John went in to wake him.

The shock of finding that Graham was not just asleep, but dead, was something John would never forget.

Fortunately, calling the doctor seemed to set everything else in motion automatically. We did not have to organize anything, only answer a few questions.

Undertakers must be used to people dying in strange places, but Graham was quite a large man, and getting his body up out of *Plain Kate* and down the path was quite difficult.

Thinking about it now I am sure Graham himself would have chuckled.

He had really enjoyed his time with us. He had been so thrilled to go out on the water, sailing. And it was obvious that he really enjoyed being with the youngsters. His one desire was to share with them all what was to him the most important thing — a personal relationship with Jesus Christ. Graham had such a down-to-earth way of talking about God that he challenged us all about how much our Christian faith really meant to us. He passed on his own unshakable belief that Jesus Christ was interested in the whole person and in everything we did. Graham himself was pleased to share the enjoyment of sailing, the enjoyment of God's creation, with young people.

He would be greatly missed.

This was quickly brought home to us by the need to take Graham's diary back to Twink, so that she could sort out all his many engagements. We left the group in the capable hands of Bosun Mike, Steve (the chief sailing instructor) and Kathy (our cook), knowing that Graham would have wanted them to go and have a really good day's sail. Then John, Cathy, David and I took Graham's Range Rover back to Bishop's Stortford.

What could we say to his wife? We felt so inadequate, so small. As Christians we knew that Graham was with the Master whom he loved and had served so faithfully. But if we felt such a sense of loss, how much greater hers would be. As we got nearer, I began to feel almost as if we were responsible, although I knew that was silly.

When we arrived, Twink's welcome was heart-warming. She must have known just how we were feeling. The wonderful strength and courage she showed was such a support to us. It was she who looked after us, she who encouraged us, and we began to feel what a wonderful privilege it was that God should have chosen the barge for Graham's final few days.

The group on board was quite stunned by what had happened. It was good to be able to share with them the Christian assurance that death is not the end, that when they die all those who have believed in Jesus and followed him in this life go to the place he has prepared for them, to be with him and to enjoy eternal life. This was Twink's faith too, and we told them of her confidence and closeness to God.

David and I both wanted to go to the funeral. It would be the day before I was due to go back to school, so we would have no opportunity for a break.

However, God seemed to know our needs and to be looking after us in a very special way. There was extensive building work being done at the school, and just after we learnt the date for the funeral I heard that the building programme was so far behind schedule the school would be closed for an extra week. Another telephone-call established that there was space for us to spend a week on a farm in Cornwall. So we were able to have our holiday after all.

But before that came the funeral. Quite often at these occasions we pay homage to the man or woman who has died. Graham had given so much to the 'rough and ready' youngsters he understood so well. We all mourned his loss. Yet the service was one of joyful confidence and praise, as we gave God thanks for a life spent in his service.

12

Wildlife on the Marshes

It was impossible to spend time on *Memory*, or to go out in the dinghies, or for a walk around the sea-wall, and not be aware of the environment. For many of the youngsters we began to entertain on board, it was so completely different from their usual surroundings that it was as if they saw things through new eyes. They found the mud exciting. They were fascinated by the tide coming in and out. They thoroughly enjoyed catching crabs over the side. And from these things it was a very short step to opening their eyes to the many other interesting things there are to see.

When school groups began to come down for field study work, the sail-loft was turned into a laboratory, with microscopes, fish-tanks, charts and blackboard. And *Ada* began to take groups out with a plankton-net or oyster-drudge, or even a beam-trawl on some occasions.

Small groups might be seen wandering onto the saltings and scrutinizing a small patch for some time. Whatever could they be doing?

Walks around the sea-wall involved studying the borrow dyke and the reclaimed land, and looking out for birds.

The village itself also provided a great deal of interesting information, as youngsters discovered the village lock-up, and the commemorative windows in the church, recalling the by-gone days of 'J' Class racing yachts and the Americas Cup.

It was especially thrilling to share some of these things with youngsters who had long ago decided that they were not interested in biology and nature study; they were just boring school subjects.

The first summer after David and I were married, we planned a week combining sailing with field study work when we would have youngsters on board from all kinds of backgrounds.

Geoff, a biology teacher with a rare gift for involving youngsters in discovering things for themselves, agreed to give us a week of his summer holiday. Going out on a walk with Geoff was like reading a thriller. We never knew what we were going to find out next. With a mix of youngsters from probation offices in the London boroughs as well as Essex Social Services Departments, a Christian youth group from Sudbury, and one or two individuals from as far afield as Bath, the ingredients were complete for a really good week.

On the programme was a walk along the northern shore of the River Blackwater to Mell Creek. This was greeted with groans and moans.

'We don' wanna go for a walk!'

'Can't we jus go up the village?'

'It's too hot — let's jus stay 'ere.'

'We wanna go sailing.'

The complaints were endless and we thought we were never going to get started. But once we got going, they all found that they were on a voyage of discovery.

Geoff's eagle eyes did not miss a thing, and he was a fascinating mine of information. Very soon, even Bryn could be heard to say, 'Look, over there! Wass that bird with those tiny babies?'

Everyone was anxious to keep up and not miss anything, because it soon became obvious that to see some things we had to be fairly quiet and really look at our surroundings.

Seeing a heron was a bonus. There he stood, so still you would almost think that he was stuffed, looking like an old man, hunched up. At last he heard a noise and took off like a jump-jet. From being so vertical, he became horizontal as he glided unhurriedly away.

We had to have sharper eyes to spot the pair of mallards, well camouflaged, on the further bank of the borrow dyke.

'Why's it called a borrow dyke?' asked one of the youngsters.

'Well, most of the sea-wall has been built up with what's been dug out of the dyke,' explained David. 'All that land there has been reclaimed from the sea — it used to be salt-marsh. The dyke provides the drainage and the sea-wall keeps the sea out.'

'Is that salt water in there?'

'Well, I suppose you would call it brackish — a mixture of fresh and salt. Look there — you can see where there used to be a creek. The indentation is still there.'

'Oh yeah. Does it belong to a farmer, then? That looks like corn or something.'

'I think that was rape. A few weeks ago it was a mass of bright yellow,' replied David.

'It looks like a six-foot-deep pile carpet now,' said James.

Geoff began to lead the way down to the borrow dyke and in seconds everyone was bounding down the side of the sea-wall, bouncing on the deep carpet of vetch which was everywhere. There was a mass of club rushes and reeds growing in the dyke and two of the girls picked some to take back to the barge. It was really quite hot, but the coot with its small family swimming in amongst the reeds looked very cool and peaceful. As we gazed at the brown, stagnant stillness of the water it was broken by the ripples left by the baby coots.

Further along, the dyke had dried out and the mud had begun to crack in the heat. One of the lads could not resist trying it out, and it was quite firm near the edge. Striding out with confidence for the other side, he suddenly came to grief, as he hit a soft patch and sank up to his knees. Did he smell when he got back to us!

We climbed back up onto the sea-wall and disturbed a pair of redshanks who 'chewpt' continuously at us until we had gone well past. They have a very distinctive call and can often be heard at night, when the tide is out and they are feeding — it is quite an eerie sound, as it carries across the marshes.

There was a real salty, seaweedy smell in the air, and looking down onto the strip of saltings between the sea-wall and the creek, the mud-holes were all wet and slimy, with old tin cans and bits of stick poking out. It was like looking down on a maze, with well-worn paths where people walked out to their mud-berths on the edge of the creek.

'Coo, look at those two birds. They're nice,' said Bryn. 'What are they?'

'Shelduck,' said Geoff. 'They're very distinctive, aren't they? When they take off, you'll notice something else about them.'

'What's that, then?' asked Bryn.

'Wait and see.'

We watched them for some time as they waddled about like little old men, leaving a pattern of footprints behind. There were some bigger footprints too — obviously some unfortunate sailor had been stranded by the tide.

'What are those sticks coming up out of the mud?' asked Sally.

'Oh, they're withies,' answered David. 'They mark the oyster-beds — didn't you see them when you were out sailing? There are quite a lot of oyster-beds in Tollesbury.'

'How do they get there, then?' asked Bryn.

'Folk who own the oyster-beds put them down. They get renewed every so often. It looks a bit like a Christmas tree plantation, then.'

'There go the shelduck,' said Geoff. 'Now, what's special about them?'

'Well, their wings are going like the clappers!' said Bryn. 'Gosh, dun they go fast?'

'That's it,' said Geoff, 'so you ought never to mistake them, even if you can't see that distinctive colouring. Are there a lot of oysters bred here then, David?'

'There are quite a number of beds — a lot up at Old Hall. But I don't know how productive they are. It takes five years, doesn't it, for them to grow to maturity? And they are quite difficult to rear.'

As we continued our walk we saw a graceful swan family, gliding peacefully along the borrow dyke. There were five cygnets who were beginning to mature quite fast. It would not be long before they got rid of their darker feathers and began to look more like their parents.

At last we reached Shingle Head Point, where we planned to sit on the shingle beach and eat our lunch. We walked across a very smelly stretch of saltings to reach what answered for a beach, and sat down to enjoy our sandwiches. It was a strange little area, where the saltings met with the shingle spit, and we could look across the river to Mersea and Bradwell, or out to the open sea. Earlier, from a distance, the nuclear power station at Bradwell had looked like a grey, mysterious monster, which seemed a threat to peace and beauty. Now that we were nearer, it just looked ugly. It might be a good landmark for sailors, but it would still be nicer without it.

Out in the deep water of the river were several large ships. Some were tankers. There was a British Rail ferry. They all looked like lazy ladies, resting and hoping to be left quietly enjoying the peace and the occasional excitement of weekend yachtsmen enjoying a race, or setting off for a week's cruise up the coast. Today there was only one solitary white sail. It is strange how empty the river is during the week. It only comes alive with sails of all colours at the weekend. Now, all we could see of the sailing boats was their masts sticking up in the distance.

We settled down to eat our lunch as we watched four oyster-catchers strutting up and down, orange beaks jabbing into the air, as if we were beneath their notice. Their red legs and black and white bodies are so striking, they remind me of clowns.

'Look at all these dead crabs,' said Daniel.

'Where? Let's see,' said Geoff. 'Ah yes. Now, are they crabs?'

'O' course they are. Look, they're perfect — this one's got all its legs and its pincers.'

'It doesn't weigh very much, does it?' said Geoff.

'No, I s'pose not. Still, I s'pose if it's been dead a long time — it must have dried out.'

'Hold it up to the sun — what can you see?'

'Well, it sort of looks like you can see through it. Like it's empty.'

'That's right,' said Geoff. 'It is empty. That's not a crab — it's just a crab cast.'

'Wha's that?' By now everyone was listening.

'Well, it's just the skin of the crab which he has cast off.'

'Why's he done that — it looks all right to me!'

'Simple. What do you do when you grow out of your clothes?'

'Buy new ones that are bigger. But where does the crab get a new shell from?'

'Grows it, o' course, silly,' said Bryn.

'But 'ow does 'e get out of 'is old one?'

'Ah, well, that's clever, that is,' said Geoff. 'You see, he extracts all the calcium from the shell — that's why it looks kind of papery and fragile. He's already grown a kind of new shell, but it's still soft and stretchy, so he makes a slit in his old shell — look here, it looks perfect, but there's a slit here — and he kind of slips out. Because he wants his new shell to be much bigger, he then takes in lots of water so that he swells up and then, after a few hours, his new shell hardens off with him all stuck round the inside.'

Everyone was listening, fascinated, including me. Usually biologists explain things by using long words that I do not understand. Not that we never used long words. When we got back to the barge and the books, we were able to look things up, but now we did not mind the 'technical' words because we understood what had happened, and we even began to understand some of the long words.

It was time to move on, for we wanted to reach Mell Creek before the tide returned. So we made our way back onto the sea-wall and continued amongst the butterflies, rich in colour. Bullfinches and yellowhammers darted about. We listened to the skylarks singing their endless song, and watched the little grey dunlin, busy at the water's edge.

106

There, out in the river, was a sailing barge, gliding gracefully through the water with all sails set. What beautiful old ladies they are!

'Is that what *Memory* looked like when she was sailing?' asked Sammy, shyly.

'That's right,' said David. 'She's lovely, isn't she? Do you wish you were on her?'

'Yeah,' replied Sammy, thoughtfully, 'but it's good being 'ere, too.'

Eventually we reached Mell and walked out onto the hard, where the old pier used to be.

'A pier! 'ere! Whatever for?' said Danny.

'The railway used to run down to here,' I said. 'There used to be a little station over there — well, just a little hut really. People used to walk out along the pier for their Sunday afternoon stroll.'

'But what would they want to build a pier for?' asked Bryn. 'Tollesbury isn't exactly like Blackpool or Southend, is it?'

'Well, when they built the railway from Kelvedon to Tollesbury, they thought that Tollesbury might become a big port on the east coast. As it happened, Harwich became the big port, and Tollesbury was forgotten, but in its heyday the railway was very busy. It was called 'The Crab and Winkle' or sometimes 'The Jam and Winkle'.'

'Why was that?' asked Bryn, who was really keen on trains.

'It used to carry shellfish up to the main line at Kelvedon, where it would quickly find its way to London. It went through Tiptree as well, where they make the jam, and that no doubt used to travel on the train. Certainly Mr Wilkin, the jam man, put up a lot of the money in order to build the line in the first place. It was a nice friendly line. You would have liked it. You could be walking across the fields and it would stop and give you a lift, or wait for Mrs So-and-So with her shopping. It would drop you off anywhere you liked, as well.'

'So where did the pier fit in, then?' asked Geoff.

'It was about a fifth of a mile long, and went right out into the deep water. That meant that a boat could unload its cargo at any state of the tide. The theory was that the goods would then be brought back along the pier and loaded onto the train. I don't somehow think many ships unloaded there, though. Things began to change too quickly, and I don't think Tollesbury could keep up. This bit of line out here wasn't open for many years.'

'What happened to the pier?'

'Well, I think rough weather might have accounted for some of the damage, but it was certainly destroyed during the war. Had to keep the enemy out.'

'So Tollesbury could well have been quite a different place, if it hadn't been for Harwich?'

'Possibly. But I don't really think that Tollesbury had the advantages of Harwich, and if it hadn't been Harwich it would probably have been somewhere else. This is a long way from the village, and the end of the pier was some distance from here. It wasn't very practical, was it?'

'I guess not,' mused Geoff. 'But it's kind of sad, all the same.'

'Come on,' said David. 'When are we going to use all this gear we've been carrying?'

We set off down the hard and looked for the right spot to dig. Geoff wanted to get a sample from the river-bed, as far out as possible, to see what animals lived at the different depths. As well as digging, we had to bang a long, hollow, square thing down into the mud, and then lift it out with the mud inside it. All the mud was then pushed out and it was possible to see the various animals at the different depths at which they lived. It looked like just a mass of smelly mud at first but, as Geoff began to sift through things and point out this and that, everyone got very interested, and longed to get everything back to the barge to look at it properly. Geoff promised us that all sorts of things would be revealed under a microscope, and we certainly believed him, because he had shown us so much that we would never have noticed.

When we finally arrived back at the sail-loft we were exhausted, but we could not wait to get the microscope out. The most amazing moment was when we were able to look at a barnacle feeding. Before, they had just been sharp things which scratched people's legs to pieces when they scrambled up onto the pontoons after swimming, or a nuisance to scrape off the hulls of the Wayfarers when they got so thick that the boats slowed down. Now they were creatures anxious to stay alive by reaching out what looked like two long tongues to catch the microscopic life that was so abundant in the water.

It had been a day to remember.

13

'There's Something Wrong with the Horizon!'

It was New Year's Day. David and I were enjoying the luxury of staying at home, and being on our own for once.

'I wonder what this year will bring?' I said.

'So much has happened in the last,' said David. 'I expect you're looking forward to things being quieter.'

I certainly was. But at that moment the doorbell rang. Two of our volunteers, Sally and Janice, stood outside.

'Are we disturbing you? We'll go away if we are.'

'No, no,' I said. 'Come in. It's lovely to see you.' And I meant it.

We were soon catching up on news, drinking tea, and watching the tide come up the road.

'We must have a walk before we go back,' said Sally. 'We need some fresh air.'

'I'll come with you,' I said, and we struggled into our coats.

We reached the bridge by the dock. Then, as I looked towards *Memory*, I had a very strange feeling.

'There's something wrong with the horizon,' I said.

'What do you mean?' asked Sally and Janice together, responding to the urgency in my voice.

'I don't know,' I said slowly, as I tried to work out what I was actually seeing.

The tide was very high, covering most of the path, and *Memory*, with her flat bottom, seemed to be sitting on top of the water. She stood out very clearly. In front of her was a small cruiser, tipped up at a very odd angle, with her bows in the air. Was it that which had attracted my attention? The boat's hull was white, contrasting with the black bulk of *Memory*. But surely *Plain Kate* ought to be next to her?

'I can't see *Plain Kate*,' I said. 'Wherever is she?'

'She must be there!' said Sally.

'But she's not. Someone has stolen her. Or perhaps she's broken loose,' I said, panic rising within me. 'But there's no wind. I must be wrong. She must be there! Perhaps she doesn't sit as high in the water as *Memory*. And yet she's not there. Come on, let's go and see.'

We hurried down the path, Sally and Janice trying to convince me that *Plain Kate* must be there. But she was not.

As I began to run and splash through the water, the truth began to dawn on me.

Plain Kate had sunk!

I could just see her davits sticking up out of the water, and the top of her coach roof, hardly recognizable. My eyes were telling my mind that she had sunk. My mind was refusing to believe it. It was impossible. How could she possibly have sunk?

'Whatever are we going to do?' I said. 'What will David say? He'll never believe us.'

'We'd better go and tell him quickly,' said Janice. 'But however could it have happened?'

'I just don't know,' I said. 'I don't understand it.'

We hurried back up the path. Tearing my boots off, I rushed into the flat.

'*Plain Kate* has sunk!' I blurted out.

'She can't have!' said David.

'She has! She's not there! You can just see her davits and coach roof.'

'Oh dear!'

It was the understatement of the year! David always remains calm in a crisis.

'Well, we'll just have to get her pumped out — though where we can find a pump on New Year's Day I've no idea. Failing that, we'll have to hole her.'

'But surely she must have a hole in her already?'

'I doubt it,' said David. 'Her hull is sound. It's not as if

111

it's *Memory* — thank goodness! We'd never get *her* up again. She'd be lost. I think I'll give Arthur a ring. He might have a pump.'

How could David be so calm about it? We were all in a panic. *Plain Kate* would have to be pumped out before the tide left her or she would spring a plank.

'Arthur thinks he may be able to find something,' said David, coming back into the room. 'I'll go down and have a look. You stay here, because Arthur is going to ring back. The other thing we could do is ring the Fire Brigade.'

'But their engine wouldn't go down the path,' I protested.

'They have a lightweight pump,' said David, as he went out of the door. 'Hang on until you hear from Arthur.'

'I'll put the kettle on. We'll have a cup of tea,' said Sally. The inevitable tea! But it gave us something to do, while we waited for the telephone.

It was not long before Arthur rang to say that he had not had any luck, but would keep trying. Then David rang from the barge to ask about the pump and to report that he had discovered the reason why *Plain Kate* had sunk.

We had turned the water off while everyone was away over the holiday period, in case of frozen pipes. Someone had turned it on again.

'But how can that have caused her to sink?' I asked.

'Someone must have left a tap turned on, or there's a burst pipe. Anyway, we'd better contact the Fire Brigade.'

Several telephone-calls later, I was waiting for headquarters to ring back. Meanwhile, Janice and Sally had already gone to organize life-jackets and the flat-backed trolley that would be needed to take the pump down the path.

When the telephone finally rang, I was almost frightened to answer in case the Fire Brigade said 'No!'

'Fellowship Afloat?' the voice at the other end asked. 'Request for assistance in pumping out sunken boat. They are on their way and should be with you any minute.'

'That's wonderful,' I said gratefully. I really did not know how to say thank you.

I hoped David was already meeting them as I grabbed my coat. It was good to see the light flashing and, as the firemen umped out and started to check their apparatus, I was really impressed with the thoroughness of their organization — just for us.

It was dark by now, and everything had to be done by the light of powerful torches and Tilly lamps. While the pump was being carefully unloaded onto the gang-plank of *Plain Kate*, hoses were being unrolled and placed in position. I wondered why they were tying the delivery-ends down.

Seeing the cockpit of *Plain Kate* full up with water brought home to me the reality of what was happening. I felt sure that God would not let anything really disastrous happen to the boat but, even so, it was lovely to hear the engine burst into life. Something seemed to be happening at last.

I soon discovered why the ends of the hoses had been secured. As the pump was switched on and the hoses filled, the force of the water was so great that they began to thrash around, and for a moment I thought they would break loose. I certainly wished I was not standing so near. But how wonderful to see all that water pouring out into the creek at 5,000 gallons a minute.

Already the tide was going down and it was soon obvious that a smaller pump would not have kept up. Considering the speed with which the water was rushing into the creek, the level in *Plain Kate* was going down very slowly.

I went to join Sally and Janice on the bows of *Memory*.

'What a lovely sight!' said Janice. 'I'd like to hug each one of those firemen!'

Sally and I laughed. We knew just what she meant.

'What would have happened if we hadn't seen her?' asked Sally.

'I don't know. She would certainly have been very badly damaged. God looks after us so marvellously, doesn't he?' I said.

'He certainly does,' replied Janice. 'If we hadn't come to visit you, and if you hadn't come for a walk with us...'

'Goodness, just look at that engine!' I said, as its glow caught my eye. 'It's red-hot. I guess it must be doing a lot of work; it's probably flat out.'

Just at that moment one of the firemen switched the

pump off, and the men took a breather.

'Best give the old girl a rest before she melts!' said one of the men.

The water-level seemed to be well under control by now, and Sally decided it was time for some coffee. She and Janice had already boiled the kettle and it was not long before we were carrying hot, steaming mugs across to *Plain Kate*.

'Well, I was right,' said David, emerging from the dark inside of *Plain Kate*. 'Someone had left the tap on, but I think water is still coming in from somewhere else — there's an outlet in the two-berth cabin which used to be used for the old bilge-pump. We need something to block it up.' He disappeared back inside.

'I think we could start pumping again,' someone said. 'The engine looks a bit cooler now.'

Soon the water was gushing out once more and then all sorts of strange things began to appear in the cockpit, as the firemen removed things in the saloon in order to get their suction-pipe down into the bilges. Thankfully the clearing-up operation would not be too bad. There was no engine on the boat, so the bilges were not full of oil and diesel, as they would be on most boats.

It was not long before the firemen were packing up their equipment and we decided that we could safely leave it until daylight to start sorting things out. We had certainly had an eventful New Year's Day!

Apart from everything being soaked in salt water, the only real damage was to the radio which belonged to our safety-launch. We had put it on *Plain Kate* for security over the Christmas holidays, but it would have been safer on *Sanderling*.

Next day, the mammoth task of rinsing everything in fresh water and then drying it out, began. The drying took a long time, but soon it was hard to find any other evidence that she had actually sunk. In fact it is still hard to believe that it really happened. And we did not even have a bill to pay as the Fire Brigade decided to waive the charge in view of the circumstances.

114

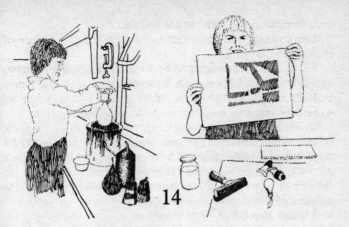

14

Paraffin Loos!

You would not think that nine girls could cause such a commotion.

'Where are the paraffin loos?' they shouted as they seethed past us and down the corridor, while we stood with open mouths, pointing helplessly, and wondering what had hit us. *Memory*'s timbers must certainly have 'shivered' as these girls shrieked through the barge.

They returned from their visit to the loos with even more shrieks:

'We're not using that!'

'We're going home.'

'You can't make us stay here.'

'Who do you think we are?'

'That's not a toilet!'

No wonder their two leaders looked exhausted. It had obviously been a real achievement to get the girls on board. We thrust cups of tea into eager hands and braced ourselves.

'Are those really paraffin loos?' asked one of the girls. 'You don't expect us to use those!'

Another outcry was about to begin. David tried to calm everyone down.

'Paraffin is what we put in the lamps,' he said, 'not the

loos. We put Elsan fluid in the toilets.'

'You call that a toilet?'

'We can't use that.'

'What do you mean?' asked David. 'It's just an ordinary toilet. It's just a bucket with a seat on. It...'

'Seat!' shrieked at least six voices.

'Seat! There ain' no seat!' said one of the girls.

'Call that a seat? I ain' sittin' on that!'

Realization dawned. The girls had been in such a hurry to inspect the loos that they had burst into the first one they had come to; it happened to be the gents' urinal!

We had to stop laughing, because they were getting more upset by the minute. Wendy was already getting her belongings together to go home.

The manner of their arrival set the tone for the week. Even if we had been a normal house with flush toilets and electric lights, they would still have complained about everything, refused to do everything — until after much persuasion they eventually joined in with twice the normal enthusiasm and entertainment value.

By now I was working full-time on the barge, being mainly responsible for the cooking, but getting involved with many other things. I had reluctantly given up teaching, feeling that it would be more appropriate to work for the Trust and be able to share time off with David. With a group like this I really wondered what I was letting myself in for.

David maintains that girls are always more trouble than boys. Well, this group certainly kept us on our toes. It often felt as though there were twenty-nine of them, not nine, and that they had been on board for ever. Of course, all the bluster and bolshiness was only a means of getting attention — and they certainly had plenty of that. For some, it was the first time that adults had taken them seriously and treated them as people who needed to be cared for.

In the best-intentioned families, contact and conversation between parent and child can easily be dominated by orders, nagging and criticism. School often provides a very similar situation. In a family where there is hurt and rejection, where parents are inadequate, the problem must be magnified.

To spend time with adults who listened to what they said, cared about them having a good time, and did not have a string of meaningless rules, was a revelation.

Our rules certainly had purpose. 'Please do not walk across the hatches, because they are rotten and you might end up in someone's cabin.' 'Do not use the gas cooker unless you are sure you know what you are doing, or we might all get blown up.'

Living together in such close proximity also highlights the importance of thinking about others before you do something, because it affects everyone else. We always warn people that it is not possible to tell a secret on board and have it kept. It is all so exciting, being with your mates, and it is tempting to have 'private' conversations in the cabins. The only trouble is that they can be heard all over the barge.

Getting to know these girls was exhilarating; it was also very frustrating. Every time we suggested doing something, they staged a sit-in strike, lined up along the kelson. With much persuasion, one by one, they would agree to have a go. Last to leave was always Wendy — and she was usually the one who enjoyed the activity the most. The truth of the matter was that everything was totally new to them, and they were scared stiff. More than anything, they were frightened of failing.

The main activity for the week was craft work, although we did go out sailing. Candle-making was a winner, once we got going. The results were not quite what you would see in the shops, but were fairly impressive just the same. A careful demonstration from David was watched with the greatest impatience: they could not wait to get started.

They were anything but careful. It was hair-raising having several girls rushing around with saucepans of hot wax, sloshing it into moulds and asking three questions at once. The favourite candle was made by using a balloon. The balloon had to be filled with water, not too much, just enough to give it a nice round shape and then, when the neck was tied, it had to be dipped in wax several times to build up a shell. Then the end was snipped off and the water squirted out, usually over someone else, and the balloon could be extracted. Next, melted dyes could be swirled inside the shell, and then it needed to be filled up with wax. This last stage has to be done very carefully or the shell goes out of shape because it gets too hot.

Needless to say, the girls made some very funny shapes. However, at the end of the week, they all managed to have a couple of candles to take home which, when lit, looked amazingly attractive. To begin with we were disappointed at their lack of care, and yet each candle seemed to have something of the character of its creator about it, and each of the girls certainly had a real sense of achievement — something very precious when failure is the norm.

By the end of the week they did not want to go home, they had had such a good time. And although we were absolutely exhausted, we really did not want to see them go. The barge had been so alive with their chatter and presence all week that, as they made their way up the path, the old lady seemed very empty and sad.

Our efforts at craft work with youngsters like these were very rewarding. Not only was it a good activity for winter weekends, it was also a good extra to have in the programme in addition to sailing, because we quickly discovered that we needed something to occupy every minute of the day in order to have a successful time.

Although these youngsters always complain bitterly that there is not enough free time, or that they do not want to do what we have planned, if they are left to their own devices they do not know what to do. Boredom seems to be a natural state for most of them. So it is especially rewarding when a craft activity has brought forth the comments: 'That was great.' 'I enjoyed that.' 'Can we do some more, after tea?' And as they share their pride in some article that they have made, it is obvious that this is an unusual occurrence in their lives.

Perhaps the most magical thing about craft work was the feeling of achievement shared with the staff and volunteer helpers who were on board. It was not just the youngsters who got a kick out of making an enamelled piece of jewellery of their own design. Not that the design is all that controllable. You can decide on the shape of the piece of copper for your pendant, and you can choose the colour of the enamels that you use, but the finished effect is more difficult to plan. There is always a moment of suspense, when someone has carefully shaken on the powdered enamel and placed the precious object in the kiln. What will it come out like? When the kiln is opened and the shape is brought out, it glows orange or dark brown. Has something gone wrong? Then, as it cools, a pattern reveals itself, and usually it is quite different from what was expected.

Forge work is a little more predictable, and the glowing of the forge fire, the ring of steel upon steel, and the physical effort, all combine to delight. A first lesson at the forge does not enable you to make horseshoes, but you can alter the shape of something that seemed solid and unchangeable. And it is usually possible to produce something — a tyre lever, or even a hammer. Making the metal red-hot is the most fun (Dad always gets cross with you if you do that with his poker) and the flying sparks as you hammer away.

A much quieter occupation can be just as successful. Fancy rope- and knot-work can result in a 'knot-board' to take home and hang on the wall. Just knowing how to tie knots can be quite an achievement, and it is great to be able to return from sailing and tie the dinghy up alongside the pontoon, knowing that the instructor will not have to re-tie it.

Tying knots can be quite absorbing, and the saloon becomes a writhing mass of rope and people, with cries of surprise when someone gets it right, and strange mutterings of 'round the tree and down the hole...' as someone struggles with the finer points of tying a bowline. It is essential to be able to tie that one in order to get the first RYA sailing certificate. But there must be an easier way to learn, and I know at least one person who never could understand what trees and rabbits had to do with tying a knot.

Those nine girls had to return home to their problems at the end of the week. So does every group that comes down to the barge. If it is a church youth group, or scout group, the chances are that most of them go back to caring homes and families. But if they have been sent down by the social services department or the probation office, they are more likely to be returning to a fairly bleak existence.

We became increasingly aware of this, as we shared with the youngsters in all our activities and began to get to know them. A weekend, or even a week, was too short a time for them to be able to form a lasting and useful adult relationship, and realize a caring, secure platform from which to tackle life. Sometimes a youngster was able to return to us; sometimes a relationship would be struck up with one of the volunteers which would continue by letter; sometimes, but very rarely, we were able to put a youngster in touch with someone back home who would offer him friendship and understanding.

We found ourselves with a real challenge. Just as we might enthusiastically ease a Wayfarer up onto a plane to heighten the crew's experience of sailing, so we had a great responsibility to heighten our group's experience of life. Ultimately, this was possible only if we were able to help them discover Jesus Christ for themselves, to realize their value in God's sight, and to avail themselves of the new start and all the resources he offers to each one of us.

But how could we show Christ to a youngster who had no idea of a loving, caring family, and perhaps little experience of love from anyone? It was very difficult. The first thing was to meet them where they were, to get to know them, and to share in the activities with them. But this was only the beginning, and we wanted to offer them so much more.

15

Colette's Story

We were expecting a probation office group on board at any moment and, as usual, making last-minute preparations. Everyone was looking forward to their arrival, as groups from this particular office always meant a great time together.

Knowing the way well by now, they were on time, and soon pouring down the for'ard hatch and bursting into the saloon with bags and bundles, excited to be here at last. A couple of lads who had been before burst into the galley, with grins all over their faces; they were obviously glad to see us again. The others followed, full of questions. They had heard so much about *Memory*; now at last they were on board. There were exclamations of delight and amazement (and a few others!), as it turned out to be not a bit as they had imagined.

There was general chaos, as we tried to sort out where everyone was sleeping, and they all seemed to be in the same cabin.

'Bags I this cabin.'

'I wanna be in 'ere.'

'Geroff my sleepin' bag.'

'Oh, can I be in this cabin? I was last time.'

The biggest problem seemed to be finding someone who knew how many of them there were. Where had their probation officer got to?

Then a girl came into the saloon with lots more baggage, and she seemed vaguely familiar. She was obviously not one of the group, but she seemed a bit young to be a helper.

121

'Hello,' I said. 'Is everyone here?'

'I fink so,' she said. She seemed a bit embarrassed and had a very strange accent, which somehow made her seem even more familiar. I asked her if she was a helper.

'Yeah, I'm a volunteer. I'm Colette.'

My mind flipped back about four years to a week in the summer of 1978 when we had a very memorable art and craft week on board. It was the only other time I had met anyone called Colette. And that accent! But no, surely it could not be the same person? And somehow I dared not ask. Instead, I asked if she knew how many were in the group, and concentrated on trying to sort everyone out.

As they were all settling in, finding their way around, having cups of tea and a quick chat about life on board, my mind mulled over the week Colette had brought to mind.

It had in fact been quite unforgettable. The week of Roger the needle, the week we had to send two girls home...

Everyone had arrived in dribs and drabs. They were just beginning to settle down, when a fight broke out in one of the girls' cabins. The noise was terrific and the language must have made even *Memory*'s timbers cringe a little.

Everyone was a bit on edge and ready to over-react, so when one of the leaders found that the door was locked, he sent someone up on deck to approach through the hatch and shouted in a loud voice, 'Open the door, or I'm coming in.'

If we had not been so worried, I think we would have all rolled around the saloon laughing.

At this point David appeared and spoke to the girls, and the door opened. Amidst tears, with everyone blaming everyone else, peace was restored. What the argument had really been about was difficult to ascertain. Wendy's cassette-player was a little the worse for wear, having been used to hit someone over the head. Colette, who was one of the group, pretended a bored indifference to the whole affair. It was nothing to do with her.

By this time dinner was ready, whereupon two girls from another cabin refused to come out, saying, 'We ain' eatin no muck — tha's just pig's food.'

122

They were obviously determined to be difficult.

Breakfast next morning was just as bad. It was quite amazing, that first morning, that they all eventually managed to get involved in the activities. Our volunteers had to be diplomats of the highest order, with an enormous fund of patience to try to enthuse and encourage the youngsters to have a go.

Sandra and Pat, the two girls who had refused to eat, were the most difficult, and had to be cajoled to do anything at all. Colette, with her pretended boredom, wore everyone's patience very thin. We began to wonder what we had let ourselves in for.

On the second day, I had just popped home after lunch when there was a ring on the door-bell. When I opened the door, the local policeman stood outside.

'Sorry to bother you,' he began, 'but do you have a group on board at the moment?'

'Yes, we have,' I said, and my heart sank. 'You had better come in. What's the matter?'

'Well, the lady in the sweet shop has had her purse taken, and her description of the girls who were in the shop at the time doesn't fit anyone locally. Could they be with you?'

From his description of the three girls involved, they were obviously Sandra, Pat and Colette. At that moment David came in. I was very relieved. I had begun to feel quite shaky.

The policeman said, 'Can we talk to the girls here? The lady doesn't want to press charges, as long as she gets her money back. If we can deal with the matter informally, it will be much better, and save a lot of fuss.'

We agreed that this was the best plan, so he contacted the local CID and we arranged for the three girls to come up from the barge. When they arrived, Colette had her nose in the air, and Sandra and Pat pretended to be most offended that we should even consider that they might be responsible.

'We don't know nuffin' — why pick on us?'

'Why you blaming us? We haven't done anythin'.'

'Have you been up into the village today?' the policeman asked patiently.

'You know we 'ave. Why d'you need to ask?'

It was obvious that they were not going to be helpful. I was cast in the role of policewoman, so that the CID men could interview the girls one at a time. No doubt the police are used to the kind of behaviour the girls gave them, but I certainly was not. Their language and obstructiveness astounded me, and I learned a few new words — though not ones I was ever likely to want to use!

The first girl to be questioned was Sandra. To every question she replied, 'I ain tellin' you nuffin', you ...'

'Now look,' said the detective sergeant, 'we're not stupid. We know that you went up to the village; we know you went into the shop, right?'

'You're so b_____ clever!'

Pat was equally unhelpful, and I was amazed at the patience of the police in the face of such rudeness. I fancied it was not the first time these girls had been interrogated by the police. To listen to Pat, you would have thought that it was the sergeant who had done something wrong.

Colette's turn came last, and she was obviously very uneasy, although still trying to appear bored and indifferent. She was a little bit more forthcoming about where they had been and what they had done, and she was really rather frightened. It was quite likely she had actually had nothing to do with the theft, but she had been a witness to it, although she would not give anything away — loyalty is a very strange thing, and no one ever wants to be a 'grass'.

On questioning Pat again, the sergeant was able to 'force' a confession, and so he took Pat and myself down to the barge to get the 'hidden loot'. We had unashamedly had someone search their cabin, but nothing appeared. In actual fact they had got rid of the purse by throwing it in the mud, so it was only the money we were looking for. Pat had stuffed it in a custard cream packet and pushed it right under her bunk, so that it just looked like a bit of rubbish. She really wanted to be arrested and was very put out not to be carried off to the police-station with sirens roaring. She was quite unrepentant, and Sandra was as much involved as if she had actually taken the purse. So we decided that they should both be sent home.

Colette was rather subdued and very sorry about the whole thing. She had been quite helpful to the police, and she was very anxious to stay and enjoy the rest of the week. Her attitude to everything changed completely. She settled down very quickly with the rest of the group. The remainder of the holiday seemed relatively uneventful, even though we attempted such things as screen-printing and tie-dying, which were completely new activities for the barge.

The climax of the week came on Friday evening, when we all gathered around the bonfire for our barbecue. Hot dogs, much singing and a talent contest provided the entertainment. One of our artist friends, who was about to be ordained, won the contest. The sight of an Anglican minister-to-be standing on his head, playing the *William Tell Overture* on a comb and paper could not be beaten.

On the Saturday morning Colette requested that she might do 'Thought for the Day'. She had got together with one or two others and written a poem, the last verse of which was:

> 'Now is the time for us to go
> And we're sad to say Cheerio
> And we'll never forget the *Memory*.
> I'd like to say on behalf of us all
> That your teaching of Christianity has
> made us realize what we could be and has
> brought us nearer to it.
> Well, we'd just like to say
> Thanks for everything.'

'Well,' said Tony, the probation officer, when everyone had disappeared to explore, 'do you remember Colette?'

'Yes, I do, but I hardly dared to believe it was her.'

'It's great, isn't it?' chuckled Tony. 'I must admit I suggested she came, and I had to do quite a bit of persuading. She's really chuffed to be here, though. She's changed such a lot. You must have a chat with her.'

Later I confessed to Colette that I had not dared believe it was really her.

'I thought you didn't remember me,' she grinned.

'I couldn't really forget you, Colette,' I said.

'I've changed a lot, you know,' she said. 'I used to be so stupid. I've grown up a lot.'

'How long have you been a volunteer with the probation office?' I asked.

'Quite a time now. I like to be with the kids. I used to be just like that, you know. I know just how they feel. They fink no one loves them and they try to make out they don't care. They act big. It's good they can come 'ere. It made such a difference you know, me coming here. I never knew God loved me till I come to the barge.'

I remembered that 'Thought for the Day'. She had been quite overwhelmed by all the love and attention she had received that week. But I had not realized how much she had been aware of God's love too.

She told me how she had started to go to a little church in Ipswich, and now taught in the Sunday school. Then she really surprised me.

'I'm married now, you know!' she said.

'Really! So what's your husband doing while you're down here?'

'Oh, he's in Canada!'

'How long's he there for?'

'I don't know. I should o' gone wiv 'im but I was too stubborn.' She grinned sheepishly. 'I know I haven't changed altogether. I'm still pretty stubborn.'

'Why didn't you go, then?'

'I didn't want to. He said he'd go by himself if I didn't go, so I said "Go on, then", and he went.'

'So what happens now?'

'I dunno. He'll have to come back. I'm not goin' out there.'

'What if he doesn't?'

'I guess God still has some changing to do to me. I fink 'e ought to come back. It's my pride, I s'pose.'

It sounded silly, but I could understand how it might have happened. She was young to be married and, as she said, still pretty stubborn. So what would happen next was anyone's guess. But at least she had given God a place in her

126

life, and recognized that she needed to learn a lot more from him.

Her commitment to the youngsters was another matter. She obviously had a great deal of understanding for them, and offered real friendship. She was a real help and a pleasure to have on board — a far cry from the belligerent, sulky Colette whom we first met. She could so easily have got into trouble at that time. Her week with us had given her a fright, but it had also introduced her to Someone who actually cared about her and loved her, and the effect had been lasting.

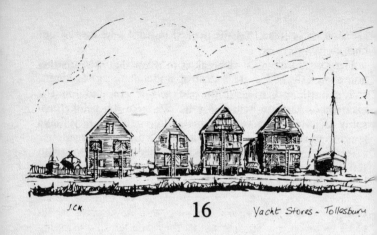

JCM

16

Yacht Stores - Tollesbury

Mudlarkers

Steve had been our chief sailing instructor for several years and felt that he would like to have a change of scenery when sailing. This would benefit the more regular instructors, as well as himself. He suggested that we should set aside a week in the summer for camping. This would make it possible to go a little bit further afield than we were normally able to manage in a day. We did not realize what an important effect this was going to have on our centre, and particularly on our thoughts about how to care for some of the more disadvantaged youngsters that we regularly had on board.

As it would be a first-time experience for us, we chose a week in the summer, when a group in their older teens and early twenties would be on board. The plan was to camp out for two nights in the middle of the week. For some reason, we omitted to tell the group of our plans, and when they arrived on board it was fairly obvious that they were not all the kind of youngsters who would respond well to camping. In fact they were not too impressed with the barge.

'Where are the showers?' was the first question.

'Sorry, we don't have any of those — unless you stand under the hosepipe!'

'Is the water soft?' asked one of the girls.

'Well, it is if you fall in over the side,' said one of our cheekier volunteers.

How were we going to break it to them that we intended going camping?

We outlined our plan for the week, emphasizing the excitement and adventure of it all. We pretended not to see some of the more worried faces, and encouraged those who looked enthusiastic.

At one stage we thought we were going to have a small mutiny on our hands but, after we had painted a frightening picture of what it would be like to be left behind on *Memory*, with no one to look after them, no Bosun to tend the toilets or make sure the barge did not sink, and how scarey it was to be alone on the barge at night, they decided that camping might be all right after all.

It seemed to call for an enormous amount of preparation to assemble all that was needed to take twenty-six people camping, making sure there was enough canvas for everyone and enough cooking equipment and food.

Inevitably all did not go smoothly, so it was to be expected that when the fleet finally arrived at their landing-place the tide was out, and the only way ashore was a trudge through the mud, carrying everything needed to set up camp. And of course it rained.

Their journey back to the barge was through thunder and lightning, and David and I were glad we had decided to 'kill the fatted calf'. They would probably appreciate a roast meal — something quite unheard-of on the barge. So a huge joint of pork and a mountain of vegetables, followed by lemon meringue pie, welcomed everyone back. The special meal, and the taste of spartan life in camp, dramatically changed the group's opinion of the barge. They now thought it was a palace!

Our enthusiasm for camping was not dampened. In retrospect it had been a great time. The following summer we decided to organize a similar week, but this time for a group which included half a dozen youngsters sent by the local authority. It was certainly quite a contrast to the previous camping group. We had a few misgivings when everyone arrived but, in the event, the camping expedition turned a good week into a really wonderful week for everyone on board, helper and guest alike.

When the time came to go home, someone suggested that we might all meet again. Perhaps it was because there was such a mixed bunch of people on board, and because during the week there quickly developed a real feeling of sharing and caring for each other.

It was something that we had not done before, and because the youngsters from the local authority were so enthusiastic it made us begin to think once more about the many deprived youngsters who visited the barge, people we did not always see again unless their social worker was able to justify another visit for them.

There was no doubt in our minds about the benefit these youngsters gained from spending time on the barge. In fact one probation office actually felt that the rate of re-offending amongst those youngsters who had been down to the barge was extremely low.

So we decided to organize a reunion weekend. It was not just for people on the camping week. We also invited all those youngsters who had visited us during the year, sent by their social worker or probation officer, to come and renew their friendships with one another and with the volunteers. And we arranged to do some fishing and some art and craft work.

Not everyone was able to come, but those who did were so enthusiastic that this was obviously the beginning of something new.

It was a quite different experience to visit the barge in winter. Gone were the hot weather, the light evenings and the days out on the water with the dinghies. Now it was dark, windy, wet and cold. But the warmth of fellowship was very real, and *Memory* fairly buzzed with all the excitement, as people caught up with one another and what had been happening on the barge.

Was this one answer to our problem of how to continue our friendship with these young people, getting to know them better, and helping them find some purpose in life?

We quickly realized that it was only a beginning, only scratching the surface of the problem. But we were certainly encouraged by the enthusiasm of the youngsters themselves.

As we talked with them and listened to their reminiscences, particularly about what coming down to the barge meant to them, the idea emerged that we should set up a kind of club which youngsters coming down from social services departments and probation offices could join. If they belonged to the club they would be able to keep in touch and we would arrange special weekends for them when they could come down and help with some of the maintenance tasks, take part in some activity, and just be together. They would also have the opportunity to come down by themselves and join a resident group, making themselves generally useful and joining in with the activities. This would be a bit like being a volunteer.

'What we gonna call us, then?' someone soon asked.

'Well, what do you think would be a good idea?'

Quite a number of ideas were forthcoming, and we finally settled on 'Mudlarkers', because that was the one everyone could agree on. It conjured up an image of grubby little urchins who had been 'mud-womping' on the saltings, as Tollesbury children called it. Well, the Mudlarkers did like the mud but, to the people who belong, what it really means is belonging to the barge and the barge belonging to them. It means a place to go where they are welcome, and where people are interested in them. It also means an opportunity for them to give something back to the barge.

As far as we were concerned Mudlarkers was an opportunity to go on getting to know the youngsters and to be able to share our faith in a relevant way. We have to earn the right to do this by caring for a youngster's practical needs and being concerned for his or her well-being.

A very important aspect of Mudlarker weekends is the 'Think Spots'. It has now almost become a barge tradition to have a 'Thought for the Day' after breakfast, and some other occasion set aside for thinking about some of the more serious issues of life. If we have a Christian group on board, this often takes the form of a Bible study and, on a Sunday, we hold an informal service on board with everyone taking part.

'Think Spots' for Mudlarkers had to be clearly relevant. There were often groans of, 'Oh, 'ere comes the religious bit!' or ''ere we go, talking about God again!'

But much of this was simply bravado, people trying to appear big in front of their friends. It was part of the act to seem not to care. But in fact they did care, and took in a good deal. Quite often during the day someone would start to talk about what had been said after breakfast, or the night before — asking questions, putting forward opinions, and showing that they had been giving things a good deal of thought themselves.

So Mudlarkers became established, and friendships began to grow between Mudlarkers and volunteers and full-time staff. It was actually quite a major task keeping in touch with these youngsters and encouraging them to come down for weekends. These visits were something they were organizing for themselves. They were not being sent down by their social worker. They were coming because they wanted to. Obviously it was hard to find the money to pay for a proper weekend, but they could save enough to contribute towards their food.

It was difficult for these youngsters to make any effort on their own. If they were asked about coming down for the weekend, or organizing travel arrangements, their response, all too often was: 'Ask my social worker. She'll sort it out.'

It was uphill work sometimes to persuade them that it was their own responsibility, that they could not always expect someone else to fight their battles for them.

Coming down to the barge as individuals joining a group, they were expected to make themselves as useful as possible, probably helping with some maintenance work on the Saturday, perhaps going out sailing with the group on Sunday.

We had always entertained individual youngsters from the local authority on board alongside church youth groups and school groups. We found that this was often more successful than having a whole group from a probation office or social services department on board. This was because the group nearly always took the youngster under their wing, cared for him and spent time with him. Best of all was the fact that they just accepted him, a situation that would not have happened 'back home' and can only be explained by the unique situation everyone found themselves in, living on board a boat in the middle of a salt-marsh, and often being in the same new learning situation.

On one occasion we had booked in a group of young people from a nationwide church youth organization, but were unable to get a full quota to fill the barge. Rather than waste the spaces, we offered them to half a dozen youngsters from social services departments in Essex and north London.

At the end of the week I apologized to some of the girls for the fact that the week had been a little different from what they had expected when they booked.

'It was great! I really enjoyed it, and those boys really taught me a lot,' one of them said. 'I've learnt a bit about how other people live this week. I think I've taken things for granted and been very selfish — living in a world of my own. Some of those kids don't have any idea what it's like to have a dad who loves them — so how can they understand about God as their loving heavenly Father? It's made me think a lot about what I believe, why I believe it, and how to share it — and not just with people who speak my language.'

Moments like this convinced us that mixing everyone up worked. And as some of the Mudlarkers began to come down a few times and got to know us, they themselves began to feel a responsibility towards the group and to identify with us in trying to give the group a good time. It was a slow process, but it was beginning to happen.

It was often more difficult with group leaders. They naturally felt a responsibility towards the youngsters they brought down, and 'difficult' youngsters were sometimes outside their own experience and therefore seen as a threat.

On one occasion a group had just established themselves on the barge when a couple of lively skinheads appeared with suitcases, having just roared down the path on a motorbike.

'What do *you* want?'

'We've come to stay, ain't we? Come for the week,' said one of the lads.

'Yeah,' said his mate. 'You 'ere for the week too?'

'Yeah,' came the strangled reply.

The two lads settled themselves on deck, lighting cigarettes, while the somewhat staggered leader went off to find David.

'There's a couple of lads just appeared. I think they're out to cause trouble. They seem to think they can come and stay!' he told David.

'Who are they?' asked David, frowning.

'I don't know, but they look like trouble.'

David went up on deck, and seeing the familiar figures of Terry and Mark, his face broke into a smile of welcome.

'Hello, Dave,' said Terry. 'How are ya, mate?'

'Fine, how are you?'

'We're OK. Be all right if we stay, will it?'

'Of course it will. We could do with a hand.'

Introductions followed, and it soon became obvious that appearances are deceptive. Terry and Mark were a real asset to the week, being really helpful and entering into all the activities with great gusto — making everything go with a swing. Terry actually learned to sail that week and went on to become one of our instructors.

Terry and Mark were really keen to catch up on all the news. Many of the Mudlarkers really identified with Tollesbury, *Memory* and Fellowship Afloat. Somehow they felt at home with us and they wanted to keep in touch.

Chatting with these two lads convinced us that it would be a good idea to send out a Mudlarker newsletter regularly, especially as it was impossible always to send personal letters. We were a little unsure of its success, because Mudlarkers are not prolific readers.

Although belonging to Mudlarkers gave the youngsters a stronger link with the barge, the feeling that they belonged to Fellowship Afloat, it did not solve all the problems. Youngsters who have very little at home often find that their stay on board has quite an effect on their lives. Sometimes this is enough to help them sort themselves out. But often they really need someone back home, someone they can be in touch with all the time.

One particular probation office began to bring a group down regularly. This meant that the number of Mudlarkers in their home town grew. Rob, one of our most faithful volunteers, felt that since he lived in the same town, there might be something he could do. As a result he opened a coffee-bar in his church — a place where Mudlarkers could go. It was open from 10 a.m. until 10 p.m. every Saturday, without fail. Our vision of local contacts in the areas from which deprived youngsters came, looked as if it was beginning to come true.

It was very hard work at that coffee-bar. Sometimes there would be no one there most of the day. Sometimes those who came would be difficult. But there was never a Saturday that was a complete and utter waste of time. Very slowly, numbers grew, Mudlarkers began to bring their friends, and the help and friendship offered through the coffee-bar began to reach people who might never see the barge.

At the same time, the germ of an idea for a holiday together, somewhere other than the barge, began to grow.

Where should we go, and what should we do?

We discovered a cottage in the Forest of Dean, whose owner did not seem at all perturbed by the thought of a dozen rowdy youngsters taking over the place.

It was surprising how insecure we all felt, away from the familiar surroundings of the barge, and the routine that inevitably takes its pattern from the rise and fall of the tides. This holiday was a complete contrast, with hills and trees, life ashore, and a new area to explore.

A programme was planned out before we went. But by the end of the first day most of the programme had been 'done', the youngsters were still full of energy, and the volunteers were all totally exhausted. Sailing obviously uses up far more energy than we had imagined.

Of course Mudlarkers grow up, and sometimes inevitably lose interest in the barge to some degree. Every so often though, a familiar face appears on the barge that we have not seen for a long time. If this happens, it is because they wanted to come back and visit a place that meant a lot to them, and tell us all how they are getting on.

One young man visited some six years after he had been on the barge, bringing his girlfriend and parents, very anxious to show them the barge where something significant had happened to him. As he put it:

'It changed my life — I could be in prison now if it hadn't been for coming down here.'

Perhaps the most exciting story of all is Terry's, that young skinhead who so shocked one of our visiting leaders. Not only did he become one of our instructors, but our friendship with him was such that, when he got into trouble and looked like being taken into custody because he had nowhere to live, we offered him accommodation and a job. Seeing him through various court appearances, witnessing the miracle of his remaining free when we were sure he would be sent down, offering him a home and friendship was a knife-edge experience. Yet somehow we survived. Eventually he actually organized Mudlarkers for us for a while, since he had such understanding for these youngsters and was able to communicate with them in a way that we probably never will.

Terry's story is a long one, fraught with problems and crises; but now he is working in a children's home, looking after very difficult and demanding youngsters and bringing to them his own unique gift of understanding. Whatever they may be going through, he has been there before.

Mudlarkers changes all the time. The youngsters are different. Some keep in touch, others we never hear of again. But there is no doubt that in some way God has met with them, and that meeting has made a difference to their lives.

17

What's Cooking?

Everyone is out sailing, the pies are in the oven, and there is an unusual lull from the normal bustle and busyness of the barge. At last the cooks can take time off for a cup of tea on deck and a quick sunbathe. For a short while it is possible to be quiet and just absorb the atmosphere of the barge.

The familiar tap-tapping of halyards, the wind and sun which will be giving the group a good sail, the birds swooping and diving over the mud, the call of the redshank — are all music to our ears.

Looking across the creek, we can see the salicornia making the usually brown banks look green with spiky, succulent shoots. The aromatic sea wormwood and pretty sea blight are much in evidence. Soon the sea lavender will be turning the marshes into a blaze of colour.

'People ask me why I give up my holiday to come down here and slave away over a hot stove,' said one of my regular helpers in the galley. 'They just don't understand. And unless they come down and see for themselves, it's impossible to explain.'

It still amazed me that people so enjoyed coming down and helping in the galley. It was hard work, and they usually contributed towards the cost of their own meals. Of course there was much more to it than the cooking, and even that was fun, simply because we were doing it together.

I certainly would not have changed my job for anything else. On the other hand, if it had not been for all the different people who volunteered their help in the galley and instructing in the dinghies, and all the different groups that came down, it would not have been so satisfying.

We were always grateful for the many different people who gave up their weekends and holidays to help us look after groups. Without them we would never have survived. It was particularly exciting when Anna (Keith and Gerry's daughter) was able to instruct — a salient reminder of how long Fellowship Afloat had been in Tollesbury.

Often the galley was teeming with people, all getting in the way. Our efforts to prepare and serve a meal for from thirty to forty people were constantly interrupted. There were people needing cups of tea. Someone wanted bacon rinds for crabbing; someone else a pair of scissors. Sympathy was required for someone in need of first aid. People came for inside information on what was for dinner. And, of course, whenever we were flat out getting things into the oven, the galley always filled up with the whole group just back from sailing. We were always very pleased to see everyone, and longing to hear the wild tales they had to tell, but we did not want to be distracted from our goal.

The most popular people were those who walked in and started on the mountain of washing-up which always results from preparing a meal.

Cooking on the barge is not like cooking anywhere else. When I first took on the responsibility of looking after the galley I worried a lot about everything. After all, I was not really a cook at all. I did not even really enjoy cooking at home. And I had to get up early every morning there was a group on board in order to be down in time to cook breakfast. But walking out across the saltings at seven o'clock in the morning and sometimes even earlier, was something so special. I might feel reluctant when I got out of bed, but once I was out in the early morning sun, or even rain, I would not have missed this opportunity to meet God's world before it was full of people.

First I would have to hunt for a wheelbarrow, then clamber up into the sail-loft where we kept our food stock and fridge and freezer, humping a crate of milk, and anything else that was needed. Then came the walk across the saltings pushing a (very often squeaky) barrow, weighted down with goodies. While Peri was with us, she would be bouncing around, pleased to be up and about, and looking to see if the tide was in, so that she could swim. Sometimes I met members of the group, too excited to stay in bed any longer; sometimes I would come down to a silent barge with everyone too tired to stir.

Breakfast was always the most hectic meal of the day, perhaps because we were not all properly awake. There always seemed so much to do all at once, serving out cereal or porridge, cooking eggs, making toast, tea and coffee.

There was usually a morning prayer meeting on *Plain Kate* while breakfast was being prepared and we always tried to organize ourselves so that one of the cooks could go to that. It was good to start the day in that way, with all the staff, talking about any problems and telling God about them, asking him to guide us through the day. All too soon it was back into the hurly-burly of the galley, getting the vegetables ready for peeling or whatever, so that we could listen to the 'Thought for the Day' in peace, usually having only just got our own cup of tea.

It was always good to share in this moment of the day. Often the thought would be quite simple; yet it had plenty to say to all of us. One morning Steve painted a picture I've never forgotten. The dinghies, he said, were like us, going in all sorts of directions. The wind blowing them around was like all the different things which influence our lives and send us off in different directions, chasing the things which we think are important. They would often be a long way from *Sanderling*, the safety-launch. And wasn't she a bit like God, keeping an eye on everyone and, seeing someone in trouble, going to help them? God can always be trusted to be there. But if help is refused — if the dinghy's crew think they can manage better by themselves — if they ignore the signals — they usually end up in more trouble.

This kind of 'thought' would speak forcibly to the youngsters because it used a situation which was now familiar, yet one they had probably not encountered before coming to the barge.

Back in the galley there was the lunch to pack while the washing-up was under way. Very soon everyone would be getting ready to sail. Then the best plan was to keep out of the way, while they got all the gear up on deck, over the stern of *Memory* and down onto the pontoons where the boats were moored. Then, with a much needed cup of coffee, we cooks could go and sit on deck and watch the departure.

We were usually sure of some good entertainment.

Sailing from the barge often seems to be a matter of catching the last of the tide. Getting away from the pontoons with a falling tide, a contrary wind and a 'green' crew is quite difficult, because the creek is so narrow. If the crew has not been well briefed, they end up in total confusion, not knowing when to duck and when to 'Lee-ho'!

People always do silly things at this point, because there are so many eyes watching, and there is so much 'advice' available. I have seen a crew rig their boat, untie it, and let it sail off, leaving them standing on the pontoon!

The most chaotic morning was when everyone got up for a half-past-six breakfast to catch the tide. *Sanderling* refused to start, taking all Steve's attention. Meanwhile, the instructors each tried to get their boat away before the tide left them high and dry. The very strong onshore wind made the whole procedure resemble a 'Carry On' film.

With boats littered all over the creek, sails thrashing, and everyone's crew knee-deep in mud, only one boat was left on the pontoons, its skipper rushing around frantically looking for a vital part of his boat that had gone missing in the general fracas. Ironically, when he finally set sail, he was the only one to get his boat down the creek while everyone else was still battling against wind and tide and mud.

The launch still refused to start and so, discretion seeming the better part of valour, a decision was made to return to the barge and start the day again. But by then everyone felt they had spent the whole day sailing, they were so tired. It would have been hard to fit all those mistakes into a whole week of sailing, let alone a day — and they had only been out an hour.

We made them all cups of coffee and reorganized our morning.

Normally, once everyone had left for sailing, we had a chance to bake cakes, clean and tidy the galley and plan the rest of the day. We were never left in complete peace, because there always seemed to be someone visiting for a cup of tea and a chat, and wanting to catch up on all the news — quite often they would stay for the rest of the day. One regular visitor always turned up once a year in his little cruising boat, mooring alongside the pontoons and coming on board for a cup of tea.

All too soon we would hear the sounds of the returning group as they poured through the hatches, full of the day's events. They would be bursting to tell all that had happened during the day, and sometimes we felt as if we had been there with them.

One particularly cold and blustery day in the autumn they returned soaking wet, with one or two people looking quite blue. Apparently, out in Mersea Quarters, the whole fleet was hit by a squall gusting to about Force 7. Within seconds it knocked over all the boats except one, whose skipper had the presence of mind to run up onto the mud. Conditions that a few minutes before had been quite exciting and exhilarating, suddenly became very frightening. With so many moored boats at close quarters, it was quite a task for Steve to get everyone on board *Sanderling* and the boats tied up for a tow home.

As we listened to all the different accounts of the adventure, one thing was clear. God had been looking after everyone. It was good to see them all safely back on board.

In the winter, people often came back to the barge freezing cold and sometimes wet, so we were experts at supplying cheering cups of tea, and getting a piping hot meal onto the table. The warmth and safety of *Memory* was savoured even more at such times.

Usually capsizes were more amusing than dramatic. One of our instructors managed to fall out of the back of the boat and, remembering the golden rule 'stay with the boat', kept hold of the mainsheet. The result was that the sails of the boat were pulled in and the boat capsized, tipping his crew into the water with him.

When the sun is shining and the day is hot, no one minds. It is all part of the fun, and makes a story to tell afterwards.

The groups I enjoyed the most were those from local authorities or probation offices, because they always showed a great deal of interest in what was going on in the galley. Someone was always poking his head through the hatches to make some comment.

'Wass that yer cookin'?'

'Thers a nice smell up yer!'

'Ugh! I ain't gonna eat that!'

Or they would tell us about the day's happenings: for instance, how a fishing expedition had gone.

'It was great — really rough!'

'How many fish did you catch?'

'None — but it was ace!'

'We were all sick — real smart it was!'

One morning, when I was making eggy bread for breakfast, one of the lads came in.

'Oh good, gypsy tust for breakfast.'

'Gypsy what?'

'Gypsy tust, tha's what we call it.'

'Do you mean gypsy toast?'

'Yeah, gypsy tust. Tha's good — I like that.'

They did not always like what we gave them to eat, though. Many of them were so used to living on chips-and-something, that they could not cope with anything else. We learnt to give them things that they would recognize easily, but even so we did not always win.

On one occasion we dished up sausages and beans, which should have gone down all right. But for some reason the lads were put out about something and, as though some tribal message had been sent round, none of them ate their dinner. Pretending to be unconcerned we took it all away, and waited to see what would happen.

The next item on the programme was a visit to the woods for some orienteering. Refusing to eat was obviously just a part of 'being difficult' because, when they got there they all refused to get out of the minibus. The group's probation officer and our volunteers pondered the wisdom of hauling them out bodily and decided to try, knowing that it was important to succeed. Suddenly, as if another tribal message had gone round, everyone complied, and really enjoyed the game. From then on the atmosphere was completely different. The next day, they ate all their dinner and wanted more: this time a minced beef tart.

Sometimes the heat in the galley was more than uncomfortable, and actually made cooking quite difficult. One day, when I had gone back to the office to catch up on some letters, I received a desperate telephone-call.

'What do you do with pastry that is all greasy? Is there a way of making it roll out?'

'Won't it roll out at all?'

'No, it just breaks up. It's so hot down here. The margarine was nearly melting when we used it.'

There was no time to make more: some other solution was needed.

'Turn it into pizza bases,' I suggested. 'Divide it into the right number of pieces, roll it out a bit and push it into the base of the tray.' That was one problem solved.

But the heat also had a drastic effect on my part of the meal. That morning I had made trifles and put them in the fridge. We took them down to the barge just before the meal, and by the time we came to dish up they had all melted.

Still, everyone pronounced it the best meal they had ever had!

Winter brought its own pleasures and problems. One particularly cold winter, we had a bird-watching weekend, when the marshes were covered with snow and were actually frozen over. On the Saturday morning we discovered that our water supply was frozen, and we were not very pleased with the Bosun. He had promised to fill everything the previous night and to bring some water-carriers down from the loft. In fact he had managed to fill only the water-boiler and two kettles. Steve went to fetch some water while David and Jeremy went off with loads of salt to see if the pipe could be unfrozen.

The pipe would thaw as soon as the tide came in, but that would not be for another three hours. Steve struggled back down the path with gallons of water, only to find they had managed to thaw the pipe, and all I could say to him was, 'Have you brought any milk?'

'Milk!' he said. 'Milk! I've just brought all this water — I didn't know anything about milk!'

I decided that it would be expedient to send someone else for the milk, and eventually we got breakfast.

The youngsters with us that weekend were mostly from Bath. They were an unlikely crowd for a bird-watching weekend, but they seemed quite keen, and they certainly enjoyed the extremely low temperatures. Unlike orthodox bird-watchers, they brought the birds home — mainly heads, but one or two whole. They had found the birds dead from the cold, and laid them out along the hatches. One was a curlew, with the long, curved beak so beautifully designed for reaching down to feed in the mud. It was the first time I had seen a curlew so close.

This haul made the weekend for the group. They probably would not have responded as well to a more normal bird-watching weekend. And it was so cold, that they spent a lot of the time in the galley, keeping us entertained. The galley is a great place for chatting, getting to know one another and often easing the way for deeper confidences.

18

Draglines, Diggers and Dumper Trucks

As I walked down the path at seven o'clock in the morning, I wanted to shout and skip. Nothing was any different from the morning before, when I had gone down to cook breakfast, and yet everything had changed.

The marshes belonged to Fellowship Afloat. They were ours!

I told the seagull, sitting on the mooring-post, but he just rose into the air and glided off over the saltings which I had just told him belonged to us. I could not resist another little skip, as I thanked God for giving us this small corner of his world to look after.

It was over two years since we had first learnt that the area of mud-berthing where *Memory* lay, along with a larger area of unspoilt salt-marsh, the four sail-lofts alongside the road, the boatyard, slip, derrick and engineering shed, were all on the market.

'It looks as though they will be purchased and developed,' David said to Keith.

'Disaster!' said Keith. 'The first thing they will want to do is move us. We're in the prime position out there.'

'I guess that's right. Still, we'll just have to wait and see, won't we?' replied David, always philosophical.

There did not seem to be a great deal that we could do about it, except pray. Rumour was rife. Another huge marina was to be dug out and the whole area 'redeveloped'. We began to feel very insecure, but we were nevertheless confident that God was in control of the situation. It seemed inconceivable that our activities on *Memory* would come to an end. At the time we were in the middle of fitting-out *Sanderling* as our new safety-boat, we had a great many bookings, a fleet of six fibreglass Wayfarers (two of which were new,) and we had *Plain Kate*, newly fitted-out with six extra berths up-forward, to accommodate extra staff. Never before had we been so busy or so well equipped.

Eventually someone asked the question that had been lurking in the backs of our minds — our secret dream.

'Why doesn't Fellowship Afloat buy the marshes?'

All the wonderful possibilities this would open up came bursting into our minds. If we purchased the marshes, *Memory*'s berth would be secure. The other mud-berths would provide an income and we could get the boatyard going again to provide local employment. We could also ensure that the salt-marsh was not spoilt and keep the hundred or so acres which were unused at present as a nature reserve, thus preserving a unique habitat. We could use the sail-lofts as sheltered workshops, a museum, a craft shop. The ideas flowed thick and fast.

But how could we raise £100,000?

We could not even begin to think in terms of such a sum of money. Our bank balance was always wavering into the red a little, and we never had any spare cash. We only ever had what we needed. It seemed to be God's way of keeping us on target. If we had had money we would most certainly have had a land base by this time — thus losing the beautiful and unique atmosphere of the barge.

At that time we were writing to a Trust, asking for another £5,000 to help us finish the fitting-out of *Sanderling*. Our first supply of money had run out as the task had taken so long, and prices risen steeply. We had never asked anyone for such an enormous sum of money before, and we were not at all sure of the reception our letter would receive. Almost as a 'by-the-way', we slipped in a very small paragraph about our idea of purchasing the marshes.

While we waited for a reply we talked the idea through with just about everyone. They all said the same thing.

'It's a great idea. I'm sure we can raise the money!'

Then we received a letter from the Trust, promising us a gift of £20,000 if we went ahead with the purchase.

We were astounded.

We were also convinced that this gift, together with the positive response we had received from everyone, was a real indication that God wanted us to buy the marshes — and that he was going to provide the money.

So we started seriously to raise the rest of the money and negotiate the purchase. We received gifts ranging from £5 to £5,000, and, when the date for completion of contract arrived, we had raised £75,000. The bank agreed to lend us the rest.

So we became God's custodians of 150 acres of tidal salt-marsh, four Edwardian yacht stores which were badly in need of renovation, a run-down boatyard and a slip with an antiquated hauling-out system.

It had been a very interesting exercise. As a charity we were not allowed to trade. We had to set up a company — Tollesbury Saltings Ltd — to administer the 'business end'. To satisfy everyone, we had to have the property surveyed.

'Where's it all gone?' said the bemused surveyor, as he gazed over a road that had disappeared under the incoming tide. The sea was also coming up behind the sail-lofts. Not a speck of salt-marsh was to be seen.

'I see now why those sail-lofts are on stilts!' he said.

We wondered why it was that we could not reduce the bank loan to less than £15,500. We were so sure God wanted us to have the marshes, so where was the rest of the money? Maybe it was his way of making sure we let things develop slowly at first, without introducing too many revolutionary ideas.

One great benefit to David and myself was being able to take over the ground floor of one of the lofts as an office, freeing up our spare bedroom! The extra space the boatyard gave us to work on the dinghies was also a great help.

We were able to set up a Manpower Services Commission Youth Opportunities Scheme. We ran this for a year, during which ten youngsters spent up to six months with us, at the end of which time most found jobs in the area. They did a lot of work: fitting-out the office, and the mess-room, building up the path to the barge, and working on the hardstanding. The highlight was the time when we had the loan of a dragline.

We were anxious to dig out the area at the bottom of the slip, which was silted up, to create a dock and quayside. A firm of building contractors generously provided us with an 22 RB dragline and a dumper truck. Suddenly the whole place seemed to be alive with activity and the roar of heavy machinery, as tons of mud were dug out to create a huge dock, and the spoil dumped around the edge of the hardstanding area, where boats could be laid up for the winter. For some reason there always seemed to be a crisis: a broken part, shortage of diesel, or a flat battery.

Once we got the piling rig, the fun really started. It was really the wrong rig for what we wanted to do: the dragline had to stand too near the pile and, if it was not exactly vertical, disaster could strike. The lads got really involved, once they started driving in the piles which formed the quayside. All hands were needed to saw up sleepers, tie them on to the dragline, and guide them into place.

One lunch-time I had escaped from the barge for a while and David and I were enjoying an unusual lull, when there was a knock on the door. Toby stood there, breathless and shaking.

'The crane has fallen in the creek,' he said. We could hardly believe our ears.

'I was coming up the path and it just began to topple over. How the driver escaped, I don't know. He leapt off at the last minute.'

'Where is it, then?' David was already out of his chair.

'At the top of the path, where the bridge is to go. I guess he was just too close to the edge. The ground just gave way.'

The sight which met our eyes when we went out to survey the damage was unbelievable. The piling-rig had missed a moored boat by the narrowest of margins. There it lay in the mud, with the crane tipped up at the oddest angle and the track facing skywards. We wondered how on earth we would get it out. If we did not manage it before the tide came in, the crane would suffer even more damage. Frantic telephone-calls, and a fifty-ton crane was on its way.

When it arrived, it did not look big enough for the job. It seemed to take an age before everything was secured in the right place — and the piling-rig had to be removed before the crane could be brought upright.

At last the task of actually pulling the dragline upright began. Inch by inch it was brought up, with stops every so often for checks and alterations to be made.

It soon became obvious that the crane was not man enough to complete the job. The dragline was pulled clear of the creek where the tide would come in, but that was as far as it could go. It was lucky we were not on spring tides, because we would have to wait a day for a larger crane to come and finish the job — and there would be another tide before then. So the dragline was left precariously perched on the edge of the path, with the crane (the kind that sits on a lorry) taking the strain.

By now it was evening and quite a crowd of interested onlookers were surveying the scene. Eventually we all went home.

Why had all this happened, we wondered? How were we going to get the quayside finished now? The recovery of the dragline would cost the building contractors thousands of pounds. They were hardly likely to provide us with another one.

The next morning we were relieved to find that the dragline and crane were in the same position. It all seemed quite safe. There was nothing to do but wait for the arrival of the eighty-ton crane. When it arrived it seemed to be a very simple job to pick the dragline up and swing it over to firm ground.

It took us a while to recover from the disappointment and the confusion of the situation. We could thank God that no one had been hurt in the accident. This was a miracle in itself, because often there were people working practically underneath the dragline. But we could not thank him for a finished quayside. It was not finished and we felt it would have been better not to have started than to end up with the quayside the way it now was.

Then we realized that there was a 22 RB dragline parked

behind the marina, doing nothing. It would cost us money but it was there! So, before many days had passed, we were back in action again. Our first dragline driver was allowed to come and drive for us, and we were able to get a piling-rig which was far better for our purposes. This time, though, we had no foreman. The driver and David had to work out the whole operation themselves — and the lads got even more involved in what turned out to be quite a feat of engineering.

Another three weeks, and the work was finished.

With the basin dug out and the quayside complete, we had the potential for more moorings in what was known locally as 'St David's Dock'. And we would be able to make better use of the slip as we cleared away the mud and silt from the bottom of the rails.

Our dearest wish was to see Tollesbury Saltings grow, but somehow God seemed to be saying 'slow down'. We did not seem to be able to pay off the bank loan, we could not afford to employ a manager in the boatyard, and all the extra workload seemed to fall on David's shoulders. We were able to provide some employment in the boatyard, as there was certainly a lot to do in the way of tidying up and organizing things. Very gradually we were able to provide slightly better facilities for customers on the saltings and to improve the hardstanding area for boats. But it all seemed very quiet compared to the excitement of buying the marshes, all the big ideas we had, and the drastic changes we had seen take place when the dragline was roaring away from morning till night.

The story of Fellowship Afloat is one of steady growth and God's faithfulness.

The three years after we purchased the marshes were a struggle, particularly financially. Our enthusiastic visitors to the barge continued to come, and our permanent staff grew to five, but in everything else God seemed to be saying 'Wait'.

Then, in the autumn of 1983, everything started to happen at once. We had tried in the past to let our engineering shed to a marine engineer — without success. Then we realized that there was a much better use for it. We found ourselves trying to set up a Youth Training Scheme in boat-building — and in this we did succeed. A generous gift helped us to fit out the engineering shed as a training workshop. Local firms offered work experience. We found a craftsman, himself a Christian who believed in the work, to supervise the project. And there were six lads in the village who wanted to join the scheme.

At the same time we were able to set up a Community Programme, also under the auspices of the Manpower Services Commission, to employ six people, including a supervisor, to renovate the yacht stores. These are listed buildings, and it made us sad to see them deteriorating. At last we had found a way of providing some employment and getting to work on this enormous task. If we had any doubts about where the money would come from for all the materials needed, we were soon reminded once again of God's ability to provide.

In November we arrived home from a week in North Wales to find the most enormous pile of mail waiting to be opened. We had recently received a gift of £5,000 towards our bank loan, and when David opened an envelope to find another cheque — this time for £4,000 — we got very excited. David telephoned Keith, while I went on opening the post.

'There's another one here for £1,000,' I shouted excitedly. '*And* one for £5,000. That's nearly all of the loan paid off. We need only another £500, and I'm sure we could find that from somewhere.'

The next morning there was a cheque in the post for £500!

A week later, Keith went to see our bank manager on other business.

'I was looking for your loan account this morning, to see what the situation was,' he said. 'But I couldn't find it.'

'I know,' laughed Keith. 'We've paid it off!'

So, as Christmas approached, we felt we ought to celebrate. In the past we had joked about the 'firm's Christmas dinner', because there had only been four or five of us. This year we had nineteen people working for us in one way or another, plus several others living locally who were involved in regular voluntary work. So we decided to have a Christmas dinner on the barge.

Twenty-five people came.

Sanderling motored up to the road to pick up all the guests — plus David and the turkey. It is not everyone who travels to their Christmas dinner by boat — or has Christmas dinner on board, come to that. It was quite an occasion, with all the traditional Christmas fare, including an enormous Christmas pudding which had been cooked for two whole days. Keith and Gerry were able to share in this occasion with us — looking back over the past seventeen years or so with thankfulness, joy and some amazement.

So many dreams had come true, and the story was by no means over.

19

A New Lease of Life

1984 was the year of the bilge-pump. Our little submersible battery-powered pump, tucked away in *Memory*'s stern, was working overtime. So too was the Bosun, because the regular need to change batteries created some quite dramatic moments.

On one occasion a youngster came up to me and said: 'It's a bit damp in my cabin.'

'Which cabin are you in?' I asked.

'The four-berth at the end.'

I went to look straightaway. It was not just a bit damp — it was two inches deep in water. This particular girl had a reputation for making a fuss and her teacher had told her not to be so silly when she had mentioned it before.

On another occasion during the late summer Steve went on board just after the tide had gone to find that everything on the galley floor had floated from one side of the cabin to the other — the water must have run out through the same holes that it entered by! That really highlighted our problem — it was not impossible that *Memory* might sink if things were not attended to.

What were we to do?

Suggestions ranged from skin-divers to floating her onto the saltings and turning her into a land base. Very soon we had exhausted all the ways we could think of to find the leak without getting underneath her — filling the bilge with dye to see where it stained the water, hanging a radio microphone in the bilges... Eventually there was nothing for it but to call in the experts — Walter Cook & Sons, the Maldon barge yard. Their advice was simple.

'We have to see her on the blocks before we can assess the situation; it will mean coming up to Maldon with her.'

Our mouths dropped open.

'She'll never make it!' We found it difficult to imagine actually moving *Memory* — she had been there so long. But surely God had given her to us and he had not shown us an alternative boat, or told us that we should not be operating any more.

So we accepted the professionals' advice. They surely knew what they were talking about, and they had no doubts that she would make it to Maldon.

The beginning of October saw frantic preparations to get *Memory* ready for her journey up the Blackwater: two reserve motor-pumps, extra access-hatches cut into the bilge, through-the-hull openings sealed off with bungs — and of course a call to the insurance broker.

Monday morning arrived and, on the first of the midday tide, came Cook's recently commissioned tug. A quick getaway was vital, and everyone raced around unshackling and dropping *Memory*'s moorings. Then the gang-plank — the final link with the shore — was pulled across.

Memory began to glide out of her berth and, before we could look round, her stern was disappearing between the moorings towards the Leavings. It was an odd feeling as we watched her go — a bit like seeing your house being moved away. After all she had been there for the last sixteen years. Those on board were equally disorientated because the familiar deck layout of *Memory*, determined by the geography of the saltings, was now the other way round.

During those first few minutes before Tollesbury dropped out of view, visits to the bilge were frequent. Thankfully, it soon became evident that our faithful submersible pump was going to keep pace with incoming water. Even when *Memory* reached the middle of the river, and the familiar swell gave everyone a rare glimpse of what it might have been like to sail on *Memory*, she took in very little.

154

CONSERVANCY

COMMUNITY PROGRAMME

BOATYARD & MUD-BERTHING

SAIL LOFT PRESERVATION

YOUTH TRAINING SCHEME

MEMORY

SHALOM

CRUISING. WORKING IN THE COMMUNITY

Back in the office, I could contain my curiosity no longer. I rang Cook's yard to see if she had made it on the one tide.

I was glad to find that they were as excited as I was and had binoculars trained to follow *Memory*'s progress up the river. She had apparently had to go aground at Heybridge, but was expected to come in that night at about 10.30.

Keith, Gerry and I went down to the quay to see her come in, peering into the darkness. What a lovely sight as she rounded the corner and crept up the river. And how exciting to go on board and realize that she was in Maldon. Normally there would be nothing odd about this experience on a boat, but for *Memory* it was an EVENT.

As soon as the tide was high enough, *Memory* was floated onto the blocks and secured. After a cup of coffee, Keith, Gerry and I left David and the others to sleep on board. They heard the most frightening chorus of cracks and bangs as the tide left *Memory* high and dry on top of the blocks. Next morning as they scrambled down through the mud to stand underneath *Memory* it was like a 'tropical rainstorm'. What a fright! From that time onwards for the next ten days, every time David went underneath, his face must have been a picture of horror — though the imperturbable shipwrights just chuckled to themselves, saying, 'We've seen worse than this — and *they're* still sailing.'

After a scrub-off, the yard set to with buckets of eight-inch galvanized spikes, bales of oakum and gallons of black jollop. At one point they shouted up and said, 'We've found a big hole here.' When they added, 'It's as big as a trap door!', no one dared to go down and look.

Before the next spring tide the yard felt they had done sufficient to keep her afloat for another ten years or so. *Memory* had been given a new lease of life. Full of gratitude and having enjoyed a very pleasant stay in Maldon, she left the blocks and, with the tide and wind under her, was soon back in the familiar surroundings of the Leavings, where she had to sit on the mud until the tide came in.

I could not contain my impatience and cycled around the sea-wall to see her. David waded ashore to tell me that they would be in by about half past nine.

Once more we watched her come up the creek in darkness, skilfully guided alongside the pier by the accompanying tug.

With *Memory* safely back in Tollesbury and the promise that she would last for another ten or even twenty years, we could not help but reflect over the last sixteen years.

What a long way we had come since those early days when *Memory* was used for only a limited number of weekends during the summer and all we had besides was a motley collection of dinghies we had begged or borrowed. Keith and Gerry's first vision had certainly materialized and grown beyond all recognition. We could look back thankfully on sixteen years of God's provision and faithfulness.

It was almost like a dream, and yet we knew that it was real. The thousands of people who had stayed on board — many of whom have their own story to tell of how they have met with God in some way and he has met their need; the material gifts we had received, and the projects we had undertaken; all were a testimony to the fact that God had and still has work for us to do in Tollesbury.

As we look into the future we do not know what surprises God has in store for us.

We have already been able to provide long- and short-term employment for a number of people; the potential is there to provide more.

We have often considered the need for long-term commitment to individuals like Brian and the need for accommodation.

If the idea is one God wants us to act on, we go ahead; if it is simply our own idea, it never seems to work. Often things happen for which we are quite unprepared. Who would have thought that we would be able to purchase the marshes!

So we look forward with excitement and expectation, wondering what God will ask us to do next.

What happened when

Although the stories in this book are roughly chronological, there has inevitably been some rearrangement to bring together events concerning a particular person or aspect of the work. For those who like to have the order of events clearly laid out, the following (selective) dates will help:

September 1967 First newsletter sent out
March 1968 *Memory* purchased
July 1969 Charitable status approved
Summer 1970 Groups begun in earnest – with a motley collection of boats
Summer 1971 Royal Yachting Association recognition for sail training
Summer 1972 David's first summer
August 1974 The oyster-smack race
Summer 1975 Brian's first visit to the barge
October 1975 The steel lighter bought in Plymouth
December 1975 David and Margaret's wedding
September 1977 Ferro-boat project begun, Brian comes to live in
November 1977 *Plain Kate* arrives, First fishing weekend
December 1977 First medieval banquet
January 1978 The memorable high tide
May 1978 *Sanderling* arrives
August 1978 Art and craft week with Colette, Graham Leavers' death
April 1979 Margaret joins Fellowship Afloat
August 1979 First camping weekend
December 1979 First bird-watching weekend
February 1980 Tollesbury Marsh project begun
April 1980 *Sanderling* launched, Easter Monday
August 1980 Tollesbury Saltings Ltd set up
October 1980 Marshes purchased
November 1980 Mudlarkers started

January 1981 *Plain Kate* sinks
June 1981 Digger work begun
1981 Youth Opportunities scheme
Autumn 1983 Youth Training scheme and Community
   Programme
December 1983 Christmas dinner for twenty-five
October 1984 *Memory*'s trip to Maldon